ENDORSEMENTS

I love the spiritual balance Joseph Z has applied to the New Testament office of the prophet. Prophecy works in agreement with God's Word, and angels are in charge of fulfilling spiritual warfare. It is simple, yet profound. I know you will enjoy Joseph's book, *Servants of Fire*.

Bob Yandian
Teacher, Author, Pastor
Bobyandian.com

Servants of Fire is an amazing contribution to an ever-growing body of work on believers partnering with the angelic realm. This is information that is meant to produce transformation; Joseph Z provides solid biblical teaching on the nature and realm of angels so that you know how to partner with them to see the transformational purposes of God come to pass on the Earth. Truly, *Servants of Fire* is a must-read, must-apply teaching for God's last-days revival remnant. For the move of God hitting planet Earth, we cannot function in mere natural human strength; Earth must partner together with the armies of Heaven to bring in the harvest of souls and nations.

Larry Sparks
Publisher of Destiny Image and Author of *Pentecostal Fire*

Joseph Z is the next big Christian author in the US. Not only are his books powerful and in a timely fashion, they are also Holy Spirit inspired. Many authors write good information, but Joseph Z writes *God information!* You can read his books for inspiration and truth; however, as you read, you will also hear God speaking to you through every chapter! *Servants of Fire* is a must-read for everyone! You will be blessed.

Ryan Edberg
Speaker, Author, and Founder of Kingdom Youth Conference

Prepare to journey through spiritual dimensions as Joseph Z guides you with the Word of God to consider the realities of the kingdom that exists beyond the veil. In the darkness of this world, you have found a tool in this manual that will empower you to speak out the Scriptures in faith, pray in the Spirit, and watch angelic assistance work on your behalf! This is not for the fainthearted; it is spiritual meat for the hungry that will supercharge your prayer life, activate God's promises inside of you, and transform any believer into the Devil's worst nightmare! So yeah, read this—your future will thank you!

Carlie Terradez
Terradez Ministries International and Global Church Family

Servants of Fire is an excellent manual for balanced, insightful, and practical teaching from a fresh perspective on the importance of angels in these last days. My friend of many years, Joseph Z, has brought us a wonderful look at the origin, current function, and future of angels in their ministry. As I read page after page, I loved Joseph's emphasis on keeping our perspective on the Word of God and keeping our focus on the Lordship of Jesus Christ as we both study and also activate angels through our prayer life. I have begun praying the Scriptures that he provides, which assist us in "authorizing and releasing angelic activity God's way" and seeing them function as *Servants of Fire* on our behalf. Highly endorse, and highly recommend it!

Carl Wesley Anderson
Author of *Love Speaks: 21 Ways to Recognize God's Multi-Faceted Voice*
Producer/director of the *Love Speaks* documentary film

I am excited about Joseph Z's latest book, *Servants of Fire*, as this is a timely word and call to action for the remnant Body of Christ. While many simply talk about all of the egregious things going on in our nation and world, Joseph articulates a God-ordained strategy and plan that is needed for us to understand how we can not only survive but thrive and take back the territory in this critical hour. This book is a must-read and will leave you equipped and ready for battle!

Todd Coconato
President of the Religious Liberties Coalition
Founder of Remnant News

Almost everywhere we look, we can see darkness on the earth and deep darkness on the people. That's why we must also be aware of the strategies, weapons, and heavenly help the Lord has given us for these epic days. Chief amongst these are the angels He has assigned to our lives (see Hebrews 1:14). We all owe a big *thank you* to Joseph Z for his new book. *Servants of Fire* will do for you what Elisha did for his servant—open your eyes to the host of Heaven that is ready, willing, and able to work with you to achieve the plans and purposes of God in this hour. *Servants of Fire* provides Scripture keys to help you activate the ministry of angels in your life and on the Earth!

Robert Hotchkin
Founder, Robert Hotchkin Ministries
Men on the Frontlines

We live in a day and age when living supernaturally has quickly gone from a luxury to a necessity. In *Servants of Fire*, Joseph Z shares how God has provided supernatural assistance for you through the ministry of angels. As you read this book, your prayer life will be strengthened, your mind will be renewed, and you will be awakened to what your life could be like if you cooperated with the angelic ministry God has made available for you. I enjoyed many things about this encouraging book, but what I loved the most is that everything is based on God's Holy Word. It is solid teaching that instructs you concerning the unseen world and helps you avoid supernatural deception.

Kerrick Butler II
Senior Pastor
Faith Christian Center

You are going to need to watch out because as soon as you read this book of amazing truth concerning the supernatural realm, your heart will hear Heaven's voice simply and clearly. Through this writing, I have found Joseph Z accurately lays out biblical truth regarding the unseen war, and it has opened my eyes to an even deeper place of God.

Gabe Poirot
Social Media Influencer
Gabe Poirot, Youtube Channel

*Secrets of
the Unseen War
& Angels
Fighting for You*

SERVANTS
of FIRE

JOSEPH Z

Published by Harrison House Publishers
Shippensburg, PA 17257

ISBN 13 TP: 978-1-6675-0213-7

ISBN 13 eBook: 978-1-6675-0214-4

For Worldwide Distribution, Printed in the U.S.A.

1 2 3 4 5 6 7 8 / 27 26 25 24 23

DEDICATION

I would like to dedicate this book to my grandparents Gene and Joyce. They were parents to ten children with me being their oldest grandchild. Their influence on me has been a source of tremendous encouragement in my journey with the Lord. Among the many memories I carry of them, a prominent and recurring one was coming into their home and finding them sitting together with their Bibles open. They loved the Word of God, and my grandmother, in particular, was a woman of prayer. At a young age, my grandparents were also a catalyst in my walk with the Lord. They would often bring me to meetings, and following we would have extensive conversations about the Lord and His Word.

They are both with the Lord today, yet they left a permanent mark on me to serve Jesus. At the time of my grandmother's passing, I had the great privilege of officiating her funeral. In the moments of reflection and processing what to say about such a wonderful person, a deep sense of gratitude came over me for all they had done to lead our family. I recalled asking her one time what her favorite Scripture was, and she replied by quoting Hebrews 12:2, "Looking unto Jesus, the author and finisher of our faith, who for the joy that was set before Him endured the cross, despising the shame, and has sat down at the right hand of the throne of God." She went on to say, with tears flowing down her face, that the joy set before Him was us.

Grandpa was a very successful businessman, and Grandma took care of the family, yet, as a result of my grandparents' faith, many people have heard the gospel around the world, ministries were supported, the poor were helped, and many were impacted by them just being them. They were people who loved the Lord and knew how to pray. I loved them dearly and look forward to being reunited in the age to come.

CONTENTS

FOREWORD

I t is my honor to write this foreword for Joseph Z's book *Servants of Fire*, a book that is intellectually stimulating and spiritually powerful—a rare mixture and a gift to those who will read it. Right up front, I want to say I believe Joseph is an exceptional prophetic voice. He is also a gifted writer, and I believe that every page of this book has something life-changing for you to ponder before proceeding to the next page.

Joseph states from the start that he was compelled to write this book as a handbook for prayer and effective spiritual living. He felt the need to do some rightsizing concerning common misperceptions about angels, who are the *servants of fire* referred to in this title. I can only say bravo to Joseph's conclusions on the pages you are about to read.

There are many common misperceptions about angels, and this is due in part to a lack of solid Bible teaching on the subject. Joseph also correctly states that religion has done a lot of damage to our understanding of angels, and in addition many cults have attempted to utilize angelic narratives to substantiate false doctrine. Joseph helps to solve this problem for us by exploring the full history and role of angels as recorded in Scripture. He covers the fall of Lucifer, and he gives us a compelling description of the mutinous angels who abandoned their God-given posts at the time of Enoch—the angels who rebelled against the authority of God. Joseph's exploration of the story of those rebellious angels and the penalty they paid for violating God's assignment to them is, for me, one of the big highlights of this book.

Joseph adeptly describes the hierarchy of angelic ministry in God's kingdom, the various roles in which angels serve, how the ministry of angels is available right now to every child of God, and how to voice-activate their assistance. To be sure, this is thought-provoking material to digest! As I read chapter to chapter, I kept thinking, *This is simply amazing—how can this book get any better?* But as I continued, I discovered truths waiting for me that were equally powerful. I am honored that Joseph asked me to read this book, and I can honestly say it is the most comprehensive material I've ever read on the subject of angels.

Get ready for an adventure! Joseph Z is about to take you on a riveting spiritual voyage that will thrill you and keep you in awe of the Lord who commands these armies of angels. And if Joseph's goal was to write a book to encourage prayer and effective spiritual living, he has certainly hit the target!

Angels are available to help you and are waiting for your voice to activate their service. As you read this amazing book, you will discover for yourself that God-sent angels are powerful agents equipped to provide a wide range of benefits to every believer, and that includes you.

Rick Renner
Author, Bible teacher, and broadcaster

PREFACE

One of the reasons this book became a reality is partly due to a visitation I had. The encounter took place after finishing a two-week series on my morning live broadcast in which I taught about prayers that release angels. Heather and I were sitting in our living room after the final teaching in that series. I said goodbye to the audience and sat back in my chair, sensing the presence of the Holy Spirit, when suddenly the room began to change. The holiness of God filled the space followed by a sense of intensity. You might say it was borderline fearful, only with an electrical charge in the air. Suddenly, a *voice spoke* with authority! This was undeniably an angelic encounter. The messenger came to share seasonal information with Heather and me regarding our personal lives, the future of our ministry, what we were to expect, and some clear orders.

Truthfully, the experience left me in tears and utterly exhausted when it came to an end. I will elaborate further on that encounter in the pages within this book. I have long believed that the way angels are depicted and interacted with is not the highest and best use of *why they exist*. They are not deities; they are not something to be worshiped or even revered. They are *fiery servants* who minister to the heirs of salvation. They are not for us to fellowship with and command to do whatever we desire. As *flames of fire* who serve the saints, it should be understood that they are not butlers, nor are they errand runners for Christians. Rather, they are *fiery servants* activated and empowered by the voice of God. You will find such help and favor when you unlock how they operate. Personally, we have had multiple encounters with what we believe were angels, only in the form of humans. This, in my opinion, is the most common way people have direct encounters with angels.

It is also essential to understand their origins, storyline, the fall of their mutinous brothers, and the guidelines they operate by. For angelic assistance to be effective, we must follow guidelines and rules of engagement. Having a better understanding of how they operate will allow you the necessary tools for a better quality of life. This book will explore not only the above information, but it will also engage angels according to the Word of God.

Summoning the forces God has provided is something many believers take for granted. It is not a matter of what you think about these *servants of fire* that matters most—it is a matter of what the Word of God prescribes. These mighty messengers and emissaries, from the kingdom of Heaven, are a powerful force designed to be activated by the believer. I have personally found much of the dialogue regarding angels has been focused on strange encounters that contradict the Word of God. When the emphasis on something is misplaced and misidentified, it causes misappropriation. When individuals don't understand the purpose of angels, how can they expect to deploy them appropriately and utilize their full potential?

I was compelled to write this book as a handbook for prayer and effective spiritual living. I hope to bring a rightsizing to common perceptions surrounding angelic encounters and to bring clarity to the purpose of angels. Some may ask, "What is the highest and best use of their relationship with us?" When properly activated, angels become a weaponized mechanism that will transform your prayer life and ultimately release the highest level of effectiveness.

An area of great importance that cannot be stressed enough is the Word of God mixed with prayer. A potent force that has been neglected by much of the modern Church. However, I believe it will be coming back with great momentum soon—out of desperation!

While writing this book, I aimed to give you, the reader, the highest and best results in prayer. You need to be armed; the way much of the Christian world has taught prayer, especially regarding angels, is misaligned and off-target. It is of such importance that we begin to recognize the need for clear angelic cooperation but not for experiences, which seems to be the focus of many of those in the prophetic movement. That is a large mistake, as we will explore in the pages ahead. Effectiveness and results, based on how the Bible prescribes prayer, are where we are headed. If you want results, you'll find them in this book. Many desire experiences filled with euphoria—far more than what is depicted in a strong biblical foundation. There is nothing wrong with experiences when in their proper place, but we must be in a place of solid discernment. This book offers guidance found in biblical truth for such experiences and tools for rightly discerning them.

There is a direct correlation between God's Word and the activation of these *servants of fire*. I trust that as you read this book, you will "take more ground" and win more battles through prayer than you've witnessed before. Angels are not arbitrary beings that just float in and out of our lives based on a whim. They are servants, *flames of fire*, potentially created out of the presence of God, *the Consuming Fire*. Angels are voice-activated, but not by your voice alone—it is your voice *carrying* or *relaying* the Word of God. We will explore this and discover how to be more effective in your prayer life. Believe me, the kingdom of darkness does not want this secret weapon and tactical advantage in your hands.

I believe this book will offer you a greater understanding of the spirit realm, the origins of angels, the way they interact with us, and much more regarding the realm of the unseen. It is my desire for you that by the end of this book, the information provided will impact your prayer life and change the course of effectiveness in your assignment!

Get ready to get results and activate the armies of Heaven— God's way!

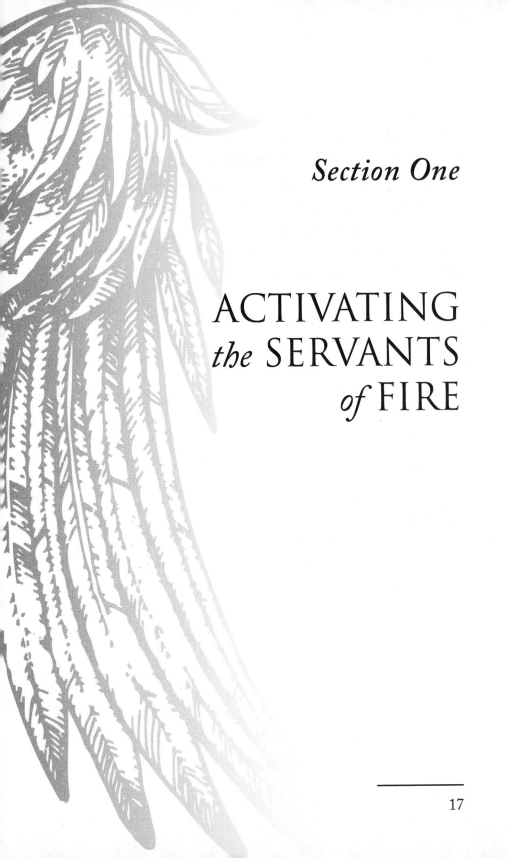

Section One

ACTIVATING *the* SERVANTS *of* FIRE

Chapter One

LAST DAYS PROPHECY
and INTERCESSION

Therefore I exhort first of all that supplications, prayers,
intercessions, and giving of thanks be made for all men.

1 Timothy 2:1

We are being plunged into the most pivotal days in history. For the rest of the world, they may feel like bystanders on a shoreline as a massive inescapable tidal wave roars over them. The Spirit of the Living God is calling right now saying, "You were born for this time—*the Last Days are here!*"

An even more accurate way of saying this would be to say, *it is the last of the last days.* All the signs point to it; Scripture and prophecy are being fulfilled almost daily. It is during this unique and intense epoch of history that more will be required from those who belong to Jesus. By more, I mean a heightened level of prayer and deeper commitment to agreeing with the Holy Spirit as agents of change.

As I discussed in the preface, there is a direct correlation between prayer, God's Word, and the activation of these *servants of fire.* Armed with these truths, we will take more ground and win more battles through prayer than we've witnessed before. Angels are servants, *flames of fire*, potentially created out of the presence of God, *the Consuming Fire.* Angels are voice-activated, but not by your voice alone—it is your voice *carrying* or *relaying* the Word of God. In this chapter, we are laying the ground for a more effective prayer life through intercession.

Intercession is—allowing the Holy Spirit to *pray through you* coupled with prophecy, which in this instance would be to "see" and "say" what the Lord is speaking. Tactically, this combination releases sharp, effective prayers with weaponized accuracy that can strike any target with maximum results. God needs your prayers; without them, His will won't automatically come to pass.

Religion would have you believe that whatever God wants automatically happens—not true. He has chosen to limit Himself to His people and have a Body by which He functions on Earth. Second Chronicles 7:14 says, "If My people who are called by My name will humble themselves, and pray and seek My face, and turn from their wicked ways, then I will hear from heaven, and will forgive their sin and heal their land." This scripture is powerful, but it was also written before Jesus arrived on the scene. Today, we have far more authority and horsepower regarding prayer than God's people did when that scripture was penned. Because of what Jesus accomplished, our great God has now given us much more authority and permission through prayer. Today, when we pray, it has the potential for earth-shaking effectiveness!

BECOME RE-SENSITIZED TO THE HOLY SPIRIT

Many are in deep need of becoming re-sensitized to the Holy Spirit because they have been **traumatized by religion.** Extended times of worship and prayer are a must for this to actually take place.

In my younger years, I would lead and participate in extended times of worship and prayer. We would worship for hours. As a youth pastor, many years ago, my entire focus was to introduce young people to the presence of God. A saying we often used, and still do today, goes like this: "Five minutes in the presence of God can do more than five years of therapy." Presence-based living creates power-based children. It was true then and it is true today! Being in a culture of worship and the presence of God causes individuals to live differently. An awareness, of who He is and the weight of His glory, does something to the human experience. It makes alterations that cannot be completed any other way.

Presence-based living creates power-based children.

ANSWERING THE FIGHT INSIDE

We are living in a culture in which *generals in the faith* and many biblical heroes from history are gone and largely remembered no more. I'm reminded of Exodus 1:8, which speaks of a new king who came into power "who did not know Joseph." Even though this great man of God rescued the very people who were made into a strong nation, they had no memory of him. If we do not know the foundation of something or how it was set into motion, we are destined to disrespect or disregard it.

The absence of discipline, guidance, heroes, and the presence of God on a regular basis causes a fight inside that brings insecurity and confusion. What are we to do to answer this fight both within ourselves and in others? We need to cultivate an encounter with God! That's the prescription!

The human experience is not a God experience.

Humanity was not created to solve these issues. No process in the human experience simply solves internal or external issues without substances, relationship crutches, the pursuit of money, or all the familiar "go-tos."

An encounter with God is desperately needed, which only comes through those who have been with Him. An amazing thing happens when the fight inside becomes answered. The ***peace that passes understanding*** will rise up, confusion leaves, and joy grows in place of your former experience. It must be said, ***the human experience is not a God experience!*** To experience this peace, you must flood your mind and emotions with His Word, increase worship, and enter God's presence. If an individual is not reading the Bible, not praying, and not spending time in worship and fellowship with God, then they shouldn't be surprised when they are depressed, cast down, sick, fearful, broken, confused, and all the other sad issues that so many are subjected to without His protection. Only God can answer the fight inside, but to encounter God there must be exposure to His presence and exposure to His people.

Prayer and intercession are a direct result of those who know the presence of God.

> *The effective, fervent prayer of a righteous man avails much. Elijah was a man with a nature like ours, and he prayed earnestly that it would not rain; and it did not rain on the land for three years and six months. And he prayed again, and the heaven gave rain, and the earth produced its fruit.*
>
> —James 5:16-18

"The effective, fervent prayer of a righteous man avails much." What a statement!

"Effective, fervent" is the Greek word ***energeō***:

1. to be operative, be at work, put forth power

    a. to work for one, aid one

2. to effect

3. to display one's activity, show one's self-operative

This says to me that we should be praying with intentional power to go to work in prayer until we get a release or see the breakthrough. To be aggressive in prayer and speak boldly when necessary!

Here is the same passage only in the Amplified version.

> *The heartfelt and persistent prayer of a righteous man (believer) can accomplish much [when put into action and*

made effective by God—it is dynamic and can have tre-
mendous power].

—James 5:16 AMP

To step into effective, fervent prayer, there must be a return to a love for the Word of God. No Word, no faith; no faith, no effective praying. This is an area of great concern in the Church today; many in this upcoming generation have a little grasp, if any, of the Bible. As a result, the question of what is right and what is wrong promotes a convoluted topic in today's society. Additionally, there is a culture war that we are being dragged into. It is a war over ideals, and it will affect the very souls of our children's children. So many before us fought for a better tomorrow only to see this present generation walk all over their sacrifice. The responsibility lies at the feet of a weak Church and a permissive society that has allowed the lawless, antichrist spirit to run wild.

Where there is no revelation, the people cast off restraint;
but happy is he who keeps the law.

—**Proverbs 29:18**

Fist-shaking or cursing the darkness has never been a productive response when dealing with a brainwashed culture. The best response is to point to something magnificent—a future of hope and a seemingly impossible vision of what we could have. I have the desire to remind people of God where they come from and what ***could be*** if they only stand up and take it! This begins with an encounter with the Living God. Prayer and times of worship are required to wake up a generation.

The Word of God Is Mission Critical

Prophecy and intercession are, simply put, **seeing** and **praying**. Commitment and focus are required in this type of prayer. Most important is a foundation on the Word of God. This is critical when training yourself to pray effectively. It is through the proper foundation and prayer that angels will respond! Through biblical praying, you are releasing the voice of God, and you are **voice activating** angelic warriors to complete their mission.

It must be understood that the kingdom of God is just that—*a kingdom!* It is made up of rules and a system by which it operates. When acting on this system of rules, you will experience a heightened level of effectiveness. Scripture is the foundational weapon, designed by God, for you to have a tangible resource in this natural world. Scripture is a physical means for engaging and reaching into the Spirit. Let me explain.

Getting a Supernatural Reaction

First Corinthians 15:46 reveals a very potent reality regarding the relationship between the spiritual realm and the natural realm.

> *However, the spiritual is not first, but the natural, and afterward the spiritual.*
>
> **—1 Corinthians 15:46**

Notice the reference to the spiritual not being first—this is a remarkable statement. Most people would ask, "What is first, the spirit or the natural?" Often many would respond by saying, "The spirit." Why? Because they know this is the realm of God; they know that we should seek first the kingdom of God and His righteousness. Many scriptural truths would point us to believe that the realm of the spirit comes first in the order of things. This scripture in context is speaking of the first Adam and the Last Adam. It explains that the first Adam was a natural man, and the Last Adam was a life-giving Spirit, straight from God. In this context, we find the principle to be ***the spirit is not first, but rather the natural is first.*** Here is one principle you can take away from this scripture. There must be an ***action*** in the natural before there can be a supernatural ***reaction*** manifested from the spirit realm.

> *There must be a natural faith action before there is a supernatural reaction.*

An example would be *healing*. We know that we are to lay hands on the sick and they will recover. Meaning, there is a natural faith action of stretching out your physical hand and placing it on a person. With this biblical, natural action of faith, a spiritual or supernatural reaction takes place. Healing will manifest in a physical body. Why doesn't it just happen straight from the Spirit? This is because the kingdom of God works through you—a natural, free, moral agent.

Similarly, salvation works through the natural preaching of the gospel. A preacher must open their mouth and release natural words by faith. Natural hearing takes place, and then a supernatural reaction happens when those who hear, believe and receive salvation in Jesus. That supernatural experience of salvation is a result of something that took place first in the natural, which induced or gave permission for a supernatural encounter. A better way to understand this would be to say that humans are the gate-keepers to what is allowed into this natural world; ergo, first in the natural then in the spiritual. We know this principle from John 3:5, where Jesus is speaking to Nicodemus saying, "Unless one is born of water and the Spirit."

This terminology *water* and *Spirit* is in reference to a person being born of a woman into the natural world. The water breaks and a baby is born. Jesus Himself had to be born of a woman into this natural world as any other entrance would have been illegal! In Jesus' explanation to Nicodemus, we see that a person must have a physical body to carry authority in this world. Without a physical body, or being born into this world, a person cannot be born of the Spirit or saved.

Below is a concept of what I mean. To experience a supernatural reaction, there must be a predicated natural action. This would be what we call a faith action. Faith actions often defy soulish logic and reason when the action takes you beyond the soulish barrier and accesses the realm of the spirit. Faith is like a bridge between soul and spirit causing a supernatural reaction. Take prophecy for example. When speaking out by faith in the natural word of the Lord, it will bypass the soulish veil into the realm of the spirit, causing a manifestation back into the natural. This is a simple picture of what I refer to as getting a supernatural reaction.

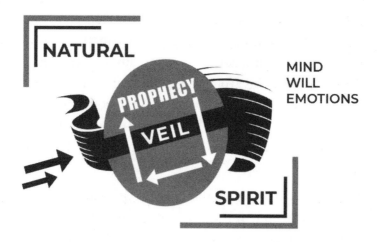

YOU ARE A GATEKEEPER

So, how does the understanding of "first in the natural then in the spirit" apply to angelic assistance? The answer is found in realizing *you are a gatekeeper*. When you, through your free moral agency, engage in praying Scripture, you are authorizing a biblical and supernatural activity to take place. Believers who are filled with faith in the written Word of God and take it a step further by speaking it out in faith, as a prayer, are *legally engaging the forces of Heaven*. It is like being in a courtroom and reading the law as it applies to the given situation. What takes place is enforcement of the law, and nothing is above the law. This reality is far greater when it comes to the principles and the kingdom laws of God.

> *I will worship toward Your holy temple, and praise Your name for Your lovingkindness and Your truth; for **You have magnified Your word above all Your name.***
>
> —Psalm 138:2

God places more emphasis on His Word than His name! This is powerful when you come to realize the magnitude of what this means! When you take His Word by faith and pray it out loud, angels spring into action.

FUNDAMENTALS OF PRAYER

Anything Scripture prescribes, when spoken by you, is something the *servants of fire* will respond to. Why? *Because the written Word of God is equal to His voice.* This is where the right kind of *prayers* described by Scripture will cause angelic forces to move into action.

> *Therefore I exhort first of all that supplications, prayers, intercessions, and giving of thanks be made for all men.*
> —1 Timothy 2:1

Let's look at the above scripture. There are *four types of prayer* listed. Throughout the Word of God there are more types of prayers, but this is a good foundation to begin with. Let's look at these four fundamental types of prayer, as each of these is tied to the Word of God and has the power to release angels!

FOUR TYPES OF PRAYER

1. SUPPLICATIONS

The Greek word used here is *deesis,* meaning "a seeking, asking, entreating, entreaty to God or to man."

And whatever you ask in My name, that I will do, that the Father may be glorified in the Son. If you ask anything in My name, I will do it.

—John 14:13-14

Praying always with all prayer and supplication in the Spirit, being watchful to this end with all perseverance and supplication for all the saints.

—Ephesians 6:18

Paul prayed often for the churches, which is an *entreating* type of prayer. Jesus *asked* God for His people to be one with Him as He and the Father were One. This type of prayer is a request made just like the woman and the unjust judge. It is a form of *asking* and *going* to the Lord for a request.

2. PRAYERS

The Greek word used here is *proseuche,* or a prayer of gathering, and it gives the sense of praying together with others anywhere. Prayers from a united people caused Peter's miraculous release from prison. Acts 12:5 says Peter "was therefore kept in prison, but constant prayer was offered to God for him by the church." These together were very effective. This is the type of prayer at work in the story of Peter being let out of prison by an angel. I find this story humorous as it speaks to the unexpectedness of answered prayer.

And as Peter knocked at the door of the gate, a girl named Rhoda came to answer. When she recognized Peter's voice, because of her gladness she did not open the gate, but ran in and announced that Peter stood before the gate. But they said to her, "You are beside yourself!" Yet she kept insisting that it was so. So they said, "It is his angel." Now Peter continued knocking; and when they opened the door and saw him, they were astonished.

—Acts 12:13-16

Here we see that the young girl, Rhoda, recognized Peter's voice and ran away out of excitement to tell everyone in the house that Peter was there, leaving Peter outside. If we read between the lines just a little bit, she was saying, "Our prayers have been answered! Peter is at the door!" Here is the funny part—they were all praying over the church, and according to Acts 12:5, they were also praying for Peter because he was in prison.

Peter was therefore kept in prison, but constant prayer was offered to God for him by the church.

—Acts 12:5

Scripture tells us how the group responded to her. They might as well have said to her, "Don't interrupt us that Peter is released from prison! That's impossible, and that's why we are praying about this very thing right now!" Or, "Don't interrupt our praying session with a miracle answer! That's not possible!" The whole incident must have made God smile. Peter didn't even know he was awake when the angel took him out of the prison, and then when he got to the house, Rhoda ran away. The people praying for his release didn't believe what they were praying for could happen, so Peter had to keep pounding on the door to get noticed!

The point can be made that when you enact prayers of agreement with others, miraculous things begin to happen, even if you don't believe it when you see it!

I recall praying with a group of friends many years ago. It was over a dear friend who had gotten caught up in an ungodly scenario. Instead of gossiping about this person or talking about the issue, we decided to come together in agreement. We held hands in a circle, about five or six of us, and we began to agree for this person's issue to be turned around. The issue was extreme and there was little to no hope we would even see this person ever again. The very next day, everything changed. A complete reversal of heart, a change of direction, and a phone call came saying they released everything involving what they were entangled in. I *know* it was the result of the prayer of agreement. It was miraculous. Upon hearing the good news, it was similar to Rhoda telling the group, "Peter is at the door!"

When you find a group to agree with, don't be surprised when the impossible happens!

3. INTERCESSIONS

The Greek word used here is *enteuxis* prayer, which addresses God for oneself or another.

Intercession often involves a conflict that must be confronted in the realm of the spirit.

Today, Jesus is our Great High Priest and intercessor. Yet we have the ability to hammer on something through prayer until it gives up or breaks through. Just as we can agree and make requests, intercession is an entirely different gear of prayer. There is a mighty aspect of *pushing through* with this kind of prayer—which goes beyond a simple request or prayer of agreement. *Intercession often involves a conflict that must be confronted in the realm of the spirit.* Jesus intercedes for you and me 24/7, while seated at the right hand of the Father. No one can intercede like Jesus! What is He praying about regarding His people? Let's look at what Scripture says about this topic. We know that in the Book of Job, Satan was able to come before the throne of God with the sons of God, or the angels. However, something awesome has happened since that time.

First, we know that Satan was operating in Adam's authority to walk with God in the cool of the day. In other words, he possessed Adam's jurisdiction rights because Eve and Adam gave those to the Devil. This, of course, is why the Devil was able to tempt Jesus with all the kingdoms of the Earth. Dominion of the Earth's kingdoms had been given to him by Adam.

Since that time, a lot has changed. Let's recall the time Satan wanted to sift Job and the Lord said, "See, all he has is in your hand." Again, this was due to Adam giving up his seat of authority. Adam's authority is why the Devil had access to destroy Job's life. God could only vouch for Job's life, but if Job could withstand the attacks, he would be justified in the end.

A similar event happened in the life of Peter.

> *And the Lord said,* "**Simon, Simon! Indeed, Satan has asked for you, that he may sift you as wheat. But I have**

prayed for you, that your faith should not fail; and when you have returned to Me, strengthen your brethren.

—Luke 22:31-32

Jesus prayed for Peter that his faith should not fail. Uniquely, this was an intertestamental period of time. Jesus was able to pray for Peter, but Satan still had the jurisdiction to make the request to *sift Peter.*

*Then I heard a loud voice saying in heaven, "Now salvation, and strength, and the kingdom of our God, and the power of His Christ have come, **for the accuser of our brethren, who accused them before our God day and night, has been cast down.***"

—Revelation 12:10

Likely this moment took place when Jesus rose from the dead and took His rightful place—seated by the Father.

*I will no longer talk much with you, for **the ruler of this world is coming, and he has nothing in Me.***

—John 14:30

*Now is the judgment of this world; **now the ruler of this world will be cast out.***

—John 12:31

*Who is he who condemns? It is Christ who died, and furthermore is also risen, who is even at the right hand of God, **who also makes intercession for us.***

—Romans 8:34

*For Christ has not entered the holy places made with hands, which are copies of the true, but into heaven itself, **now to appear in the presence of God for us.***

—Hebrews 9:24

*Therefore He is also able to save to the uttermost those who come to God through Him, since **He always lives to make intercession for them.***

—Hebrews 7:25

*For we **do not have a High Priest who cannot sympathize with our weaknesses, but was in all points tempted as we are.***

—Hebrews 4:15

The above scriptures refer to why the Devil cannot come and request (using Adam's authority and permission) to sift God's kids anymore! Jesus is the Last Adam, and He took back the access once given to the Devil by the first Adam. Neither trials like the ones Job had to endure, nor the way Peter was sifted, are options on the table like they once were. Jesus slapped that system around and took the reins back. Today, the Devil has access through the mind and by persuasion. In order to have access to tempt an individual, he needs their agreement and permission. Regarding Jesus' part, He labeled that door *access denied!*

Lucifer never had a tempter. He fell on his own doing—sin was found in him. As a result, he is not redeemable; no one tempted him, therefore, there was no one to rescue him from or no one to punish him. He became "self-aware" and wanted worship, glory, and all of his egotistical ambitions. Adam and Eve had a tempter—Satan.

Jesus likewise, only in an entirely different field of significance, found *there was no intercessor for Him!* He had to discover His own righteousness to sustain Him while tempted by the Devil. Jesus realized Adam failed, mankind failed, and even Abraham wasn't going to make the cut, so God had no one to swear by—so He swore by Himself in a covenant. Dear reader, we should take a moment and thank God for His goodness!

Jesus was sustained by His own righteousness; this overqualified Him to become the ultimate intercessor!

> *He saw that there was no man, and wondered that there was no intercessor; therefore His own arm brought salvation for Him; and His own righteousness, it sustained Him.*
>
> —Isaiah 59:16

Today, He sits at God's right hand making intercession for us. By making intercession for us, He is there to intercept the "accuser" of the brethren, who accused the children of God day and night. God must have heard it when Adam had given his keys and access to the "accuser." When Jesus returned to Heaven with the keys

Adam gave up, it must have been wonderful. Can you imagine Adam walking over and hugging Jesus for what He did?

Jesus' intercession is an intercession to stop the Devil. Jesus is seated by the Father as an eternal reminder that we are saved and we are in Him. This brings us to the point of intercession for the people of God. There is no ministry of intercession; there is, however, the ability to intercede, which was made available for all believers.

Intercession Is a Prayer That Brings Real Change

Prayer and intercession is a powerful weapon, a higher form of intensity, in which believers actually throw the authority God gave them around in the realm of the spirit.

> *Likewise the Spirit also helps in our weaknesses. For we do not know what we should pray for as we ought, but the Spirit Himself makes intercession for us with groanings which cannot be uttered.*
>
> —Romans 8:26

Intercession doesn't take "No" for an answer. Intercession prayers—mixed with faith, Holy Spirit-led commands, and praying in the Spirit—say to the *mountain* or to the *fight*, "No, you move!" Romans 8:26 listed above says, "The Spirit Himself makes intercession for us with groanings which cannot be uttered." When going deep into prayer and intercession, there is a place in the Spirit where you can tap into that groaning. Through these Holy Spirit prayers for the Church, we can join in with Him and intercede. Sometimes, you will not know what it is you are praying for by intercession. You might be praying for someone on the other side of the world, and all you know is you are joining with the Holy Spirit praying in tongues and agreeing with what He wants to be accomplished. He needs you more than you realize. *Intercessory prayer is giving God a natural voice, through you, to speak with authority and declare His will.*

One practical prayer of intercession is to pray to the Lord of the harvest asking for laborers. God needs you to intercede on behalf of a dying world. Intercession is a *go-between* prayer. It steps in and makes tactical requests for those who need to hear the gospel and you know you cannot be the one. Families are sometimes the hardest ones to reach because of familiarity. Praying to the Lord of the harvest to send laborers is a wonderful intercession, as it permits the Lord to act in a natural arena. When you pray and make requests or allow the Holy Spirit to pray through you with tongues and groanings, you are giving the Lord permission to have His will done on Earth as it is in Heaven.

> *Therefore pray the Lord of the harvest to send out laborers into His harvest.*
>
> —Matthew 9:38

Xerxes

Queen Esther's appeal to Xerxes was a form of intercession, but it was really Mordecai who was the intercessor. In a sense, Mordecai was the one who initiated Esther's action to save her nation. It was a form of sending laborers out into the fields as Jesus said. Laborers go where you cannot. Mordecai knew what needed to be done, so he interceded by influencing a laborer—Esther.

> *So it was, when the king saw Queen Esther standing in the court, that she found favor in his sight, and the king*

held out to Esther the golden scepter that was in his hand.
Then Esther went near and touched the top of the scepter.

—Esther 5:2

The background is important to realize the gravity of what Esther was risking. King Xerxes had a very unreliable personality. Gracious, kind, and given to sudden acts of rage and outbursts, he could become fiercely terrifying. This is commonly thought to be the same king personified in the movie *300* as the enormous god-king who fought with those three hundred Spartans, which history knows as the Battle of Thermopylae.

Three hundred Spartans held off an enormous Persian army by positioning themselves at the Hot Gates, a narrow passageway into their lands. (An interesting little-known historical possibility is that the Spartans were actually Jewish.)

Xerxes was notorious enough to make modern cinema because of his larger-than-life manic antics. An example of his behavior comes from history at a time when his enormous army was marching from Sardis to an area called Abydos. An important harbor of the day was located where he had built two bridges. Each bridge reached roughly 1,300 meters across. However, before Xerxes' army could utilize the bridges, a storm rose up and destroyed them both! History says Xerxes was enraged and had those responsible for building the bridges beheaded. A colorful addition to this story is that it's been said the furious king had fetters thrown into the strait and ordered for the sea to receive three hundred whiplashes! He also went as far as to have the sea branded with red-hot irons and commanded his soldiers to shout at that same water.

Esther was supposed to lay her life on the line with this same king. Her life was on the line with a madman who had breathtaking anger-management issues. However, it was her act of intercession that saved an entire nation.

4. GIVING THANKS

The Greek word used here is *eucharistia*. It conveys gratefulness and worship with gratitude to God. Gratefulness is when it's always on your lips to praise God!

> *Let the saints be joyful in glory; let them sing aloud on their beds. Let the high praises of God be in their mouth, and a two-edged sword in their hand, to execute vengeance on the nations, and punishments on the peoples; to bind their kings with chains, and their nobles with fetters of iron; to execute on them the written judgment—this honor have all His saints. Praise the Lord!*
>
> —Psalm 149:5-9

Praise is in the prayer spectrum and causes spiritual movement. Notice what happens here in Psalm 149. Singing praise leads to governmental authority! A conversation could definitely be made that this is in reference to praise and the written Word of God. We know Scripture is referred to as the sword of the Spirit, and here we see the combination of those two leads to justice and governmental change. Praise mixed with the Word of God creates a space of authority, which is an honor for all His saints!

CHAPTER ONE QUESTIONS

1. What does "becoming re-sensitized to the Holy Spirit" look like to you?

_____

_____

_____

_____

2. After reading this chapter, what steps would you take to help yourself or someone answer the fight inside?

_____

_____

_____

_____

3. How are you applying the Word of God in this critical time?

_____

_____

_____

_____

4. How can you get a supernatural reaction over something you
   are praying for?

   _____

   _____

   _____

   _____

5. What are the four types of prayers listed in this chapter?

   _____

   _____

   _____

   _____

Chapter Two

THEY OPERATE AMONG US

And of the angels He says: "Who makes His angels
spirits and His ministers a flame of fire."
Hebrews 1:7

Your entire life has been involved in an unseen cosmic war that began before time itself. *The conflict is territorial*, the stakes are eternal, and all of it involves you more than you might realize. This conflict rages daily and will only increase as we find ourselves closer to the end of the age.

Effects of this unseen drama are observable in the natural world through deteriorating moral standards, political turmoil, and growing geopolitical tension between nations. Families, co-workers, friends, and strangers you walk past in life are all directly impacted by the *invisible drama* playing out even as you read the pages of this book.

As time moves along, tomorrow's children are being persuaded at this very moment to fall deeper into a *dark system* that has a beginning birthed by rebellion. This dark system is specifically marshaled against the kingdom of God. As a result, the environment, which once held much higher respect for decency and the things of God, has been radically altered and continues to be so. Culturally, we are witnessing a rapid deterioration of what once was. New generations are not likely to experience the same days of peace that the former generations enjoyed. What would seem, only a few years ago, like strange or foreign events to ponder are the norm today. Perversion, corruption, and cultural deterioration seem to be the main talking points given to us via a highly developed *infotainment culture.* Pandemics, outbreaks, war jargon, economic challenges, famines, and so much more are now *normal news.* Not to mention the daily issues you and your family are confronted with routinely.

UNNATURAL CIRCUMSTANCES

Without some form of intervention, the outcome looks very bleak. As an onlooker, it would be easy to think everything transpiring around the world is purely the result of natural circumstances. However, nothing could be further from the truth. In all reality, there is *an entire realm you cannot see*—an unseen arena impacting your daily life in dramatic ways. To the uninitiated, this may seem outlandish or even mystical. Yet, it is a greater reality than the one you currently know! The reason for this is that this natural world did not create the realm of the spirit. Much the opposite is true. Spiritual substance, or the voice of God speaking from the realm of the supernatural, is what created this natural world. You might say the spirit realm is the *parent force* to the world we live in. Reality is only understood through what we can perceive with our five senses, but it is vital to know the greater truth is the one we cannot see with our natural eyes. The stakes are high because we are only in this natural arena for so long—then it's over. We will transfer to the greater reality for all eternity!

A war between good and evil has raged since the rebellion of fallen angels, and it continues today. This war is in the realm of the unseen, but remember that it is the greater reality, and it impacts our lives in unimaginable ways. Regarding all that we don't fully comprehend or entirely understand, it is very encouraging to know that God has not left us unarmed and defenseless. In all actuality, *we have quite an advantage.* Just as the unseen realm is influencing the world around us with darkness, there is another side to the issue.

God has not left us unarmed and defenseless.

On the right side of this unseen battle, a more significant, potent force is awaiting engagement. It is an unrivaled power for good. This force I'm speaking of is a combination of two agencies—*angelic servants and believers* who walk in biblical authority. It might be better understood to say it this way: *most angels are not nearly engaged or utilized to their full capacity and original design.* This is an issue that tragically lies at the feet of God's people. Sadly, most believers do not know what is available to them. As a result, many suffer the consequences, wondering why God didn't do more to help them. All along, what they didn't know was hindering their effectiveness.

Gnawing questions rise in the hearts and minds of so many who feel as if God didn't intervene, and it is disheartening. Those who have a sense that *something didn't happen* that should have happened are not incorrect; there may have been angels who were right there watching—only unable to engage at the highest level.

You Were Made for War!

Your life is a much more potent force than you might realize. Why? Because you can alter your sphere of influence! The Lord God of Heaven and Earth has given you the ability to modify the narrative in the natural and spirit realm.

If we, as believers, knew the extent of what was available to us through angelic forces, we would utilize the profound advantages they provide. After all, the Word of God teaches us in Hosea 4:6, "My people are destroyed for lack of knowledge." Another way of saying this would be: *what you don't know can hurt you.* It is time for you to understand how to engage in angelic assistance! You are needed in this conflict! Your life and the lives of those around you will begin to change when you start marshaling these heavenly agents (who are waiting for you to do so) into service.

> *Are they not all ministering spirits sent forth to minister for those who will inherit salvation?*
>
> **—Hebrews 1:14**

Forces of Heaven are waiting for you to utilize them.

These ministering spirits, sent to serve the *heirs of salvation,* operate by a specific set of rules—directed by how you pray and the manner of obedience in which you walk out your assignment for the

Lord. As fascinating as it might be to understand, the reality is that these forces of Heaven are waiting for you to utilize them. They are standing at attention for you and waiting for their "marching orders."

> *Do not forget to entertain strangers, for by so doing some have unwittingly entertained angels.*
>
> —Hebrews 13:2

Through each circumstance that we traverse, these unseen messengers and servants are present. Although our natural senses are not equipped to identify them, it does not alter the reality of their presence. Angels see what you are doing; they are beside you and your family. Present in circumstances, nearby, and in every scenario, they are there. While operating as heavenly *emissaries,* these *servants of fire* are on call! Never sleeping, never tiring, fulfilling the desire of God, and waiting for their marching orders. Both fearsome and kind, these fiery representatives are out to fulfill the desire of the great God of Heaven. They are witnesses to the *testimony of Jesus* and serve to see that His kingdom comes and His will is done on earth as it is in His kingdom in Heaven.

It is highly possible, even likely, that you have personally run into angelic messengers on more than one occasion. The thought of it is really sobering when embraced. Taking it seriously that they are around you at this very moment, even while you are reading this page, is essential as it will give you a sense of responsibility to engage them properly. Why are they around, and what would make them have any interest in you? Because *you are made in God's image and likeness.*

Scripture teaches us clearly that *God does not give aid to angels,* but He does give aid to the seed of Abraham (see Hebrews 2:16).

Meaning, they are created to serve God and His children. You are made to be served by angels, as you are made in God's image and likeness.

Psalm 8:4-5 says that man was made a little lower than the angels. However, the actual Hebrew word the translators used was *Elohim,* a Hebrew word translated as "God" more than 2,600 times in the Old Testament and designates the one true God.

> *What is man, that thou art mindful of him? and the son of man, that thou visitest him? For thou hast made him a little lower than angels.*
>
> —Psalm 8:4-5 KJV

Angels are committed to you, as you are made in the image of God, and God delights in you. Think on that for just a moment—you are made a little lower than God! You are placed above angels in rank and authority. Your very existence has placed you there. Even unbelievers, who do not know the Lord, have more authority than spiritual forces, including angels, because although they are not in God's kingdom they are made after Him. This is a clarifying point when considering why God and angelic forces can't just do whatever they want, whenever they want. It is due to free moral agents (people) being influenced by forces other than the kingdom of God, resulting in the gates of Hell taking territory. When the righteous don't know who they are or what they possess, darkness has an advantage. This of course is why it is highly imperative that you are learning about angelic forces and how you should relate to them. We will continue on this train of thought in greater depth.

---

*It might shock you to discover
that your prosperity is one of the
things that angels attend to.*

ANGELS ARE COMMITTED TO YOUR WELLBEING

It is worth noting that angels are not only here to serve the heirs of salvation, but they do so out of a desire to accomplish that which pleases God. It might shock you to discover that your prosperity is one of the things that angels attend to.

> *Let them shout for joy and be glad, who favor my righteous cause; And let them say continually, "Let the Lord be magnified, who has pleasure in the prosperity of His servant."*
>
> *—Psalm 35:27*

> *Bless the Lord, you His angels, who excel in strength, who do His word, heeding the voice of His word. Bless the Lord, all you His hosts, you ministers of His, who do His pleasure. Bless the Lord, all His works, in all places of His dominion. Bless the Lord, O my soul!*
>
> *—Psalm 103:20-22*

Notice Psalm 35 states that the Lord has pleasure in the prosperity of His servant. That means you! God delights in you doing well, increasing, having value, and enjoying your life! What a concept! What's even more remarkable, according to Psalm 103, angels do His pleasure—*your prosperity!*

When discussing angels, the authority must always remain with the Word of God.

As an act of doing what pleases the Lord, angels are committed to your prosperity. This of course goes well beyond the popular culture's idea of prosperity. *God takes pleasure in you doing well in every area of your life,* and His angels are committed to seeing it happen—what a wonderful realization!

RELIGION'S DAMAGE TO ANGELS

Religion has done a lot of damage to our understanding of angels. It seems it's either a dismissive understanding of them and their existence or just as ineffective as the hyper-mystical beliefs pushed by religious superstition. Parts of religious institutions nearly worship angels, while cults utilize angelic narratives to substantiate their false doctrine. When discussing angels, the authority must always remain with the Word of God. If the Word of God doesn't teach it, say it, or give an example of it, what we are left with is speculation and sensationalism. By reading the Word of God, we will have a proper view and understanding of these very present entities. The Word of God clearly shows us that they are very real and very powerful agents for the benefit of believers.

It is fascinating that *the Devil couldn't beat the Church* when it was formed by the Holy Spirit in Acts 2, so he did the next best thing he could do—he joined it. How? Through *religion*. As a result of the Devil's influence on religion, he has been able to do tremendous damage to the reach of the gospel, but also to the reputation of God. I believe he has additionally invented false narratives regarding angels that have weakened their effectiveness among believers. What a person believes will impact the results they receive; this is the reason darkness would attempt, wherever possible, to spread a false narrative about angels. Darkness is outnumbered at least two to one by angels loyal to God; additionally, the forces of evil, fallen angels, and all powers associated with it don't stand a chance in a direct conflict with the forces of Heaven.

The Devil couldn't beat the Church when it was formed by the Holy Spirit in Acts 2, so he did the next best thing he could do—he joined it.

And war broke out in heaven: Michael and his angels fought with the dragon; and the dragon and his angels fought, but they did not prevail, nor was a place found for them in heaven any longer. So the great dragon was cast out, that serpent of old, called the Devil and Satan, who deceives the whole world; he was cast to the earth, and his angels were cast out with him.

—Revelation 12:7-9

As Revelation 12 explains, the Devil and his angels don't stand a chance against Michael and his angel armies. What these dark powers have left is a *false flag campaign*. They must get free moral agents to be unaware of and apathetic to all the Lord God has provided for them through Jesus. The biggest issue regarding spiritual forces is the lack of discipline and biblical cooperation with the forces of Heaven. Further, the chronic issue is that the kingdom of darkness is more disciplined and organized than the Body of Christ. Allow me to reference something Rick Renner brings out in his masterpiece on spiritual warfare titled *Dressed to Kill*.

"The devil is so serious about doing damage to humanity that he deals with demon spirits as though they are troops!" —Rick Renner

---

Rick points out the Greek word *kosmokrateros* to describe what Ephesians 6:12 (KJV) identifies as "rulers of the darkness of this world." Paul tells us that the Devil deals with his dark legions of demon spirits as if they were military troops. Rick goes on to say regarding the Greek word *kosmokrateros*:

It is a military term that has to do with discipline,

organization, and commitment. The devil is so serious about doing damage to humanity that he deals with demon spirits as though they are troops!

He puts them in rank and file and organizes them to the hilt. Meanwhile, the average Spirit-filled believer often doesn't stay in one church for more than one year at a time!

Yes, we do have more authority than the devil has; we do have more power than the devil has; and we do have the Greater One living in us. The Church of Jesus Christ is loaded with heaps and heaps of raw power. But at this particular time, that power is disconnected and disjointed by a Body that lacks discipline, organization, and commitment! As Christians, we have no power shortage, nor are we short of God-given authority. We simply have a great lack of discipline, organization, and commitment. In order to change this, we must buckle down in the local church and begin to view ourselves as the troops of the Lord! Once we match the discipline, organization, and commitment that the enemy possesses in his camp, we will begin to move into the awesome demonstration of God's power![1]

Dear reader, you are so vital to the highest and best use of angelic activity. You are about to see what this means and how it will impact your life as well as the life of your loved ones.

I think Rick's insight is very revealing. Becoming disciplined and organized is what we must consider in our own lives. We possess everything we need for victory and to overcome the power of darkness; however, what is lacking is commitment. When done appropriately, the potent force of divine assistance will come into action for you.

RIGHTLY UNDERSTANDING ANGELIC WARRIORS

The kingdom of darkness has had *religion* providing assistance to it through wrong understanding. Suppose what we know about angels is relegated to chubby babies on birthday cards or cupid-looking little cherubs shooting arrows for love. Angelic warriors are diminished to just weak little beings with no power to crush the assaults of darkness.

Many strange tales are told regarding angels, such as religion's popular saying, "The reason your loved one died is God needed another angel in Heaven." Sadly, this causes some to believe that loved ones who die and leave earth will turn into angels. The infiltration, of mysticism or new age type of belief, suggests angels are euphoric entities causing unique sensations in the air.

Some prophetic-type ministries even go as far as saying they see angels all the time, sometimes manifesting the strangest things, such as feathers or gold, etc. Something popular for a while in circles I was aware of was the concept of *women angels* that would walk through a room and healing would break out or some other manifestation. The common issue with all of these is that none of it is represented in the Word of God. Now please understand that unique things can and do sometimes happen, and it's certainly not my desire to be critical. However, we need to have a solid foundation to stand on, and if something strange happens and a unique encounter should manifest leading you to believe it was angelic, remember the words of Paul the apostle:

> *Now these things, brethren, I have figuratively transferred to myself and Apollos for your sakes, that you may **learn in us not to think beyond what is written,** that none of you may be puffed up on behalf of one against the other.*
>
> —1 Corinthians 4:6

REAL ANGELS GLORIFY JESUS

If you have an outright angel encounter, please realize it should point to and give all glory to Jesus Christ. Anything else should always stand firm on the exhortation given by Paul "to not go beyond what is written."

In the pages ahead you're going to receive a practical understanding in regard to how to *engage angels*, how to *activate them*, their *origins*, the cosmic battle, and ultimately how they will benefit your life as a believer!

There are rules of engagement, as John discovered in the Book of Revelation. Many of the biblical figures who encountered angels were dramatically impacted by the experience. Remember, they are constantly among us. Angels are near you right now protecting, advancing, and making sure all is well.

CHAPTER TWO QUESTIONS

1. What are ways you can shift the environment around you?

_____

_____

_____

_____

_____

2. Have you ever felt that someone you encountered was an angel?

_____

_____

_____

_____

_____

3. How do you think angels help people on a normal basis?

_____

_____

_____

_____

_____

4. What areas of your spiritual life can you bring into order?

_____

_____

_____

_____

_____

5. What are false understandings of angels that you have heard of or been taught? How does that affect your thoughts today toward angels?

_____

_____

_____

_____

_____

6. If you've had an angel encounter, did that angel bring glory to Jesus?

_____

_____

_____

_____

_____

Chapter Three

RULES *of* EFFECTIVE ENGAGEMENT

God is Spirit, and those who worship Him
must worship in spirit and truth.

John 4:24

A fascinating realization comes into focus when the perspective of flesh and spirit comes into view. This means, the realm of the spirits or spiritual entities carries a vantage point of superiority to the realm of the flesh. Job 4 really drives the point home when we are able to eavesdrop, through Eliphaz, on the Devil as he was rhetorically talking to himself. His main complaint was *the weakness and uselessness of mankind,* making the argument (to himself) that mankind is flesh and not spirit. His argument was, "Why does God even regard these frail beings?"

WE WALK BY FAITH, NOT BY SIGHT!

Remember Elisha and his servant when they were surrounded by an army? In 2 Kings 6:16, Elisha's words to his servant were, "Do not fear, for those who are with us are more than those who are with them." His servant was in a panic because the city was surrounded by the enemy, and in this unique moment Elisha asked the Lord to open the eyes of his servant. Astonishment and boldness came upon the servant due to seeing into the realm of the spirit! At the end of verse 17, it says, "Then the Lord opened the eyes of the young man, and he saw. And behold, the mountain was full of horses and *chariots of fire* all around Elisha." Much like Elisha's servant, if we were to see into the realm of the unseen, we would be astonished as well and walk with much greater boldness regarding the things of God. Remember, however, *blessed are those who do not see and yet they believe.* God loves it when we believe without seeing! It is important to know that spiritual entities such as angels and demons can see the contrast of the spirit realm running parallel to the natural realm at all times. Forces of light and darkness each continuously are witnesses to the power available in the spirit realm. Faith is our mechanism for contending in these unseen arenas. We walk by faith, not by sight!

The time Gabriel appeared to Zacharias when announcing that Zacharias would be the father of John the Baptist is a great example of how angels, from the realm of the spirit, see what are sometimes limitations or the unbelief of those bound up in the weakness of this natural realm. Zacharias was full of unbelief. When he asked the question, "How shall I know this?" he and his wife were old in age. It was not a response of faith; rather, it was him questioning everything Gabriel was saying. As a result, Gabriel told him that his mouth would be shut—*this* is how he would know. Now, this is a point of interest for the simple fact that Zacharias was about to ruin a miracle that God was about to release due to years of prayers and spoken prophecies. So, both as a sign and a utility to rescue the miracle from being sabotaged, Zacharias's mouth was shut.

And Zacharias said to the angel, "How shall I know this? For I am an old man, and my wife is well advanced in years." And the angel answered and said to him, "I am Gabriel, who stands in the presence of God, and was sent to speak to you and bring you these glad tidings. But behold, you will be mute and not able to speak until the day these things take place, because you did not believe my words which will be fulfilled in their own time."

—Luke 1:18-20

Take special notice of Gabriel's response here. He says, "I am Gabriel, who stands in the presence of God." As if to say, "I see God and all His majesty all the time. Why are you questioning this message? Mortal!" It was a tiny glimpse into the way spiritual beings view the natural. Spiritual entities also know the horsepower available to us from the realm of the unseen. They also witness the tragic level of distraction and lost potential in each generation regarding lost opportunities in the realm of the spirit.

Another example of spirit versus natural comparisons is the time Jesus referred to seeing Satan fall like lighting. Jesus shared with the disciples a glimpse into the supernatural splendor and glory through the comments He made. He knew the level of awesomeness the realm of the spirit contained. He even would say with irritation, "How long will I put up with you, unbelieving generation!" Wow! That is very revealing, as it is my suspicion that He was saying, "If you would simply *believe*, we could pull everything we need out of the spirit realm into the natural realm and accomplish anything!"

*Then the seventy returned with joy, saying, "Lord, even
the demons are subject to us in Your name." And He said
to them, "**I saw Satan fall like lightning from heaven.**"*
—Luke 10:17-18

You see this point driven home upon Jesus' comment, "I saw
Satan fall like lightning." The disciples were excited about casting
out demons. This was one of the first times the disciples had seen
a supernatural manifestation that took place through their own
hands. Jesus was letting them know that there is a greater glory that
can be seen. Not to mention that casting out demons is basic. Jesus
goes on to say in verse 20, "Nevertheless do not rejoice in this, that
the spirits are subject to you, but rather rejoice because your names
are written in heaven." That is something to rejoice over!

One more example was the instance when Jesus spoke to
Nathanael about being under the fig tree. This word of knowledge
blew Nathanael away! Jesus was amused by this and commented
further. It was as if Jesus was saying, "You like this? But wait,
there's more!" Again, among many things that can be taken away
from this tremendous conversation between Jesus and Nathanael is
the comparison of how awesome the realm of the spirit is compared
to the natural. Jesus was in essence saying to Nathanael that as
dazzling as it was to experience that word of knowledge, what was
going to be revealed in the realm of the spirit would far surpass this
encounter—angels ascending and descending on the Son of Man!

*Jesus saw Nathanael coming toward Him, and said of
him, "Behold, an Israelite indeed, in whom is no deceit!"
Nathanael said to Him, "How do You know me?" Jesus
answered and said to him, "Before Philip called you,*

when you were under the fig tree, I saw you." Nathanael answered and said to Him, "Rabbi, You are the Son of God! You are the King of Israel!" Jesus answered and said to him, "Because I said to you, 'I saw you under the fig tree,' do you believe? You will see greater things than these." And He said to him, "Most assuredly, I say to you, hereafter you shall see heaven open, and the angels of God ascending and descending upon the Son of Man."

—John 1:47-51

Spirit Force

Isaiah 31:1-3 gives us a little more insight into the spirit versus the flesh perspective. Here we see God talking through Isaiah referring to the Egyptians.

Woe to those who go down to Egypt for help, and rely on horses, who trust in chariots because they are many, and in horsemen because they are very strong, but who do not look to the Holy One of Israel, nor seek the Lord! Yet He also is wise and will bring disaster, and will not call back His words, but will arise against the house of evildoers, and against the help of those who work iniquity. Now **the Egyptians are men, and not God; and their horses are flesh,** *and* **not spirit**. *When the Lord stretches out His hand, both he who helps will fall, and he who is helped will fall down; they all will perish together.*

—Isaiah 31:1-3

Notice how *flesh is talked down to*. God is saying that those who think Egypt is so mighty need to understand that Egypt is merely flesh—speaking of their abilities. This point is driven home even further with statements such as, "Their horses are flesh and not spirit." As simple as this sounds to natural human beings, it isn't simple to the Lord or the armies of Heaven. What can be challenging is how the rules of engagement operate in a spiritual fashion versus the natural setting we live in every day. Naturally speaking, *we want to see results* in the way we want to see something happen. More often than not, our way is disconnected from God's way. Man's desire for the miraculous can often be *similar to a desire for magic*. What many people want to see when they pray is similar to magic in that they want results that make no sense, yet blow the mind. Popular culture has trained us all to think this way, but it is not God's way.

Again, yes, miracles happen, and He wants to perform miracles more than we want to experience them. It is, however, a cultural manifestation or corporate oneness that engages what God has already provided through Jesus! Meaning, when we are gathered together in His name, He is in the midst of us. When we come together in one accord, He is present. Later, we will look into New Testament prayers, but it is my suspicion that the greatest untapped resource is the Body of Christ together as a largely united front, in unison, as one in principle, and in faith standing on the Word of God. The "secret sauce" is found in the Body of Christ coming together in faith on a corporate level more than a prayer meeting.

At a young age and after spending many hours in prayer, again and again, one of the frustrating things I had to work through was wanting prayers to be answered my way. I wanted to see something shocking take place instantly when I prayed. This mindset, although not incorrect to a certain point, is incomplete without understanding the realm of the spirit.

Faith is the main currency within the kingdom of God!

Now, can miraculous, instantaneous things manifest? Of course, they can and sometimes do! Yet, what must be understood when it comes to the dynamic relationship between the natural realm and the spirit realm is that there is a relationship based on permission—a concept that is very mighty when grasped. When it comes to the rules of engagement (with the kingdom of Heaven) there must be an activation point for the kingdom of God to manifest on Earth. When referencing the kingdom of God and the kingdom of Heaven, there is a difference. The kingdom of Heaven is a location, and the kingdom of God is a system. The greater the system of God is in action, the more the kingdom of Heaven can manifest and activate in this natural world. Jesus even said when teaching the disciples to pray in Matthew 6:10, "Your kingdom come. Your will be done on earth as it is in heaven." This is accomplished by free moral agents, such as yourself, acting on what the Word of God prescribes. It must, however, be activated by faith, not simply by going through the motions. *Faith is the main currency within the kingdom of God!*

Coming back to the idea of spirit and flesh. The spirit realm is the *source realm* or *parent force* of all-natural creation; therefore, all things natural have a connection to the realm of the unseen.

Another point of understanding is regarding how creation was formed—*spoken words!* God *spoke* and it *was.* This is vital to know, as creation began with words, and it still responds to faith words today. Any faith action from the natural realm is an act of permission or activation. We might say that faith actions induce supernatural manifestations from the realm of the spirit. We hear things like, "Angels are so powerful," or "The Spirit of God is so mighty," and yet we see nations in disaster and the world falling apart with little to no empirical impact from our prayers. It can make anyone wonder what the deal is. Why are we told the Spirit, angels, and God are so mighty, and yet all this challenge?

It is due to the spirit realm being *suppressed* by the natural realm. Human beings are the gatekeepers! If we were to cooperate with the realm of the spirit, not just as an individual but corporately, we would see tremendous results—Old Testament-type miracles would manifest on the scene! Jesus Christ is the same yesterday, today, and forever! The issue is bad teaching, a lack of revelation, and a lot of cerebral processing with the kingdom of God rather than a united *faith-filled Body* giving tremendous permission for the Spirit of God to release what has already been done in the spirit into the natural realm.

Human beings are gatekeepers!

The spirit realm is by far the greater authority; we just haven't seen that to its fullest. This is due to a lack of proper engagement, religion, and many of the non-biblical approaches to the way we

---

pray and the way we unite. There is a glass we see through dimly; there is an understanding even when it comes to a prophetic revelation about the realms of the spirit, but it is limited. We know in part, we prophesy in part, and we see through a glass dimly. My answer to seeing through a glass dimly is that we should polish the glass! The glass represents the soul or veiled area between the spirit and physical realms. Belief is fostered in this space for the good or the negative. Belief is soulish and must be developed by the Word of God. What you believe can hinder what you receive.

Every believer should polish the glass!

Third John 1:2 says, "Beloved, I pray that you may prosper in all things and be in health, just as your soul prospers." In simpler terms, this means that you will receive to the level you can believe! Whatever your soul is trained in is what your soul will experience, and ultimately what you will allow or deny regarding what can manifest in the natural realm from the spirit.

> *Be sober, be vigilant; because your adversary the devil walks about like a roaring lion, seeking whom he may devour.*
>
> **—1 Peter 5:8**

As a result, permission is what is required to gain access to the natural world from the realm of the spirit.

Both God and the Devil are territorial.

In these last days, it's easy to see how the influence of evil can gain access to a fallen culture, especially in a world that does not know the Lord. Darkness, in a sense, must preach its message in order for human beings to engage with it. Once humans engage with the influences of darkness, the act of permission is eventually given through agreement, much like Adam and Eve, who allowed the serpent's voice to persuade them in the garden. The taking of territory begins when an individual leaves the influence of darkness unchecked in their personal life. This same impact of evil can lay hold on a *corporate level*, leading to a society blinded by darkness.

Whoever controls the thought life of a free moral agent, controls their trajectory, and ultimately their destiny.

THE TERRITORY OF FREE MORAL AGENCY

All spiritual beings must work through rules and laws—even God. He created the very fabric of the universe, and as a result of speaking things into existence He will not alter what He has ordained. Much like darkness preaches its *agenda*, the light of God must be preached. Romans 10:14 teaches us clearly, "And how shall they hear without a preacher?" Preaching the Word of God to humanity is vital as it allows the hearer to authorize God to begin working in their life. Each human being is a *free moral agent*, meaning they are responsible for their own life, decisions, the direction they will go, and what influence they allow or alienate. Darkness has an advantage in that humanity is very carnal, born into evil, and is affected by the original sin of Adam and Eve. Thus, those in the world are born into sin and desperately need a Savior.

What a person believes and practices matters greatly! It is a severe thing to enter eternity without ever understanding this reality. Jesus must be made Lord of a free moral agent, or they will step into a crisis eternity without any reprieve.

EMISSARIES OF PERMISSION

Ranks of angelic messengers and warriors are *hard-wired* to do the job they were created to do—to serve the heirs of salvation. However, their job is not automatic and requires the *law of permission*. As interesting as it may sound, angels are *beings* of permission; they operate by rules. Exactly how we just walked through free moral agency's relationship to darkness and light—angels are no different.

It can be a startling discovery for some when the realization takes place that these *servants of fire* function most effectively based on the level of your *obedience* and the right use of *prayer*. In other words, what you are doing versus what you are called to do can have an impact on angelic effectiveness. It is a mighty truth to embrace that the way you pray majorly impacts angelic effectiveness in your life.

Your life was designed by God to succeed. He desires success for you in your calling. It takes a commitment to follow the high calling of God on your life. Jesus had this experience when He was finished with the forty days of fasting. At the end of this time in the wilderness, once He had overcome and defeated the three temptations from the Devil (who tried to dominate Jesus), angels were waiting to minister to Him.

ANGELIC ASSISTANCE

One circumstance stands out clearly in my memory. I was driving out an evil spirit that had taken hold of a young lady immersed in witchcraft. The deliverance session was dramatic! It was a heightened experience for me as this evil spirit was attempting to attack people in the room. Being much younger at the time, I didn't really know what to do. The only thing I did know was that I was filled with the Word of God. Authority rose within me as I recalled scriptures such as Psalm 91:11, which says, "For He shall give His angels charge over you." Also, Psalm 34:17 says, "The righteous cry out, and the Lord hears, and delivers them out of all their troubles." Continuing, Psalm 34:7 says, "The angel of the Lord encamps all around those who fear Him, and delivers them." Standing on the scriptures that were bursting at the seams inside of me, I called out in faith for angels to assist me—wow, did they ever!

This young lady had demonic voices speaking through her and was displaying freakish strength. However, the moment I called out for *angelic assistance* from a heart flooded with the Word of God, an invisible force body slammed this violent, demonized person to the ground! She was suddenly pinned to the ground like a starfish. Unable to move but still snarling like an animal, the young lady was bound to the floor. From this position we were able to cast the demons out of her quickly and without any violent outbursts. As amazing as this moment was to me, I am convinced the demonstration of power was due to having the Word mixed with faith in my heart! I called out for the help of angels, but my heart was full of authority firmly based on the Word of God. I spoke out, not as someone with a good idea, but rather as someone with a revelation. I knew what the Word said was true, so did that evil spirit, and so did the angelic forces who were very present in that scenario.

On another occasion, we were driving into a storm when suddenly it seemed as if we drove straight into a tornado, and then lightning hit the car! Just as we drove into this intense wind, with rain blowing directly sideways and zero visibility, I shouted out in faith, "In Jesus' name!" It was all I could get out when the lightning hit us directly—it was sparking off the sides of the windshield. As this deafening noise was taking place and electricity was popping and sparking off the windshield corners, we suddenly blasted out of the storm on good roads again. It was as if nothing had happened! We were completely safe and there was zero damage to the vehicle or us. When this situation happened, it felt as though there was a supernatural bubble around us. Angels had intervened! This was due to a heart filled with the Word of God mixed with faith. When I called out to the Lord, faith was present based on the Word of God, and we were rescued from certain harm.

Often it could be that angelic forces are standing by and are not able to engage the enemy or situation you are facing as they haven't been authorized by *the rules of engagement*. Not that they do nothing or cannot do anything—it may be that they are simply limited.

Of great interest is understanding what angelic forces are capable of. Let me explain. When you engage the forces of Heaven, the way God has prescribed it there is not much that can withstand what these *servants of fire* are capable of accomplishing on your behalf. As stated earlier, they are not incapable, they are just limited. "Limited to what?" someone might ask. Well, they are limited to what we have already identified as the rules of engagement. Before explaining this further, let's gain a little understanding of what angelic capability looks like, beginning with Jesus' reference to calling on twelve legions of angels.

ANGELIC POWER IS ASTONISHING

> *Or do you think that I cannot now pray to My Father, and He will provide Me with more than twelve legions of angels?*

—**Matthew 26:53**

I am grateful to Rick Renner for his observation regarding the above scripture. Let us consider that one legion (a Roman military number) represented 6,000 soldiers. In the above passage, Jesus referenced that He had at His disposal *twelve legions* of angels. By doing a little bit of math, multiplying 12 by 6,000 equals 72,000. Jesus was saying at that moment He had, at minimum, twelve legions or 72,000 angels on standby. Saying the words, "He will provide Me with more than twelve legions," shows us that 72,000 was the minimum number that would rush to His aid.

Angelic power and capability are astonishing. Here is what I mean. From examples in other parts of Scripture, let's look at what angels have done. Isaiah 37:36 shows us that one—only one angel, all by itself—destroyed 185,000 men in one night. If one angel is capable of wiping out 185,000 men in one evening, what could a legion of 6,000 angels do?! The answer is one legion of angels could annihilate 1,110,000,000 men. To be clear that is one billion, one hundred ten million men!

Let's take this angelic *body count* of 185,000 and multiply it by 72,000 angels, which was the number of angels Jesus said was available to Him on the night of His arrest. When we do, we find that there was enough combined strength at Jesus' disposal to have annihilated at least 13,320,000,000 people! Again, to be clear that is thirteen billion, three hundred twenty million people. That would be the equivalent of destroying the population of the world at least two times! The combined strength, in this number of angels Jesus referenced, is a force no civilization has ever experienced in the history of the world.

> *But you have come to Mount Zion and to the city of the living God, the heavenly Jerusalem, to an **innumerable company of angels**.*
>
> —Hebrews 12:22

The numerical exercise we just looked at above does not account for all the angels. Hebrews 12:22 states that there is "an innumerable company of angels." With this in mind, the power of Heaven's forces is beyond comprehension. Each member of the armies of Heaven has a deep respect for Jesus, not only as their Lord and One whom they obey but due to His obedience and what He went through for mankind. Think about His level of discipline, obedience, and sacrifice that He was willing to pay for us and for the pleasure of His Father. His ability to call on the above-mentioned *tsunami of angelic warriors* reveals that if Jesus had made this choice, God would have honored it.

Jesus was the hinge pin to our eternal damnation or redemption. Do not think for one second that it wasn't a temptation for Him to pass up on the sacrifice He would have to make, which was *required* for our salvation. Sweating blood in the garden demonstrates the immense pressure He was enduring. Not only was He dreading the crucifixion, but there was the magnitude of taking on the sin of the world. A scenario of unspeakable horror—Jesus was willing to pay it all. Philippians 2:8-11 states:

> *And being found in appearance as a man, He humbled Himself and became obedient to the point of death, even the death of the cross. Therefore God also has highly exalted Him and given Him the name which is above every name, that at the name of Jesus every knee should bow, of those in heaven, and of those on earth, and of those under the earth, and that every tongue should confess that Jesus Christ is Lord, to the glory of God the Father.*

Had He not taken on this dramatic sacrifice and action, He likely would have returned to the Father and left us under the oppression and control of the Devil. More was at stake in these moments than the average believer might realize. The *servants of fire* knew this as they witnessed it all firsthand from the spiritual side of events. As witnesses to the events leading up to and post-crucifixion, the angelic hosts understood the scope of what was truly at stake.

> *Who, in the days of His flesh, when He had offered up prayers and supplications, with vehement cries and tears to Him who was able to save Him from death, and was*

heard because of His godly fear, though He was a Son, yet
He learned obedience by the things which He suffered.
—Hebrews 5:7-8

It was due to Jesus' radical obedience that we see the redemption of all those who call upon His name. Jesus is Lord because of what He accomplished on the cross, fulfilling the will of His Father in Heaven. Again, the forces of Heaven witnessed this, and it created reverence among the angels.

When understanding *the rules of engagement*, it is vital to know that Jesus has the undivided allegiance of the remaining forces of Heaven. *Servants of fire* only serve Jesus; they know the meaning of the words Jesus quoted in Luke 4:8 (NIV), saying, "It is written: 'Worship the Lord your God and serve him only.'" *Servants of fire* who left their proper place of service unto the Lord should be referred to as servants of *strange* fire. For these ones are no longer servants of the *sacred fire* directly from God. To engage angelic forces in prayer and to influence your life and journey requires understanding where their allegiance lies—at the feet and service of the One who now has a name above all names! Lining up with His Word through prayer and dedication causes victory and the alignment of these heavenly forces to fight on your behalf.

HERE ARE THE RULES OF ENGAGEMENT

1. **You must be in covenant with God through Jesus Christ.** Now, this is not to say angels don't help the unsaved or those who are outside the kingdom.

However, they are keenly in tune with those who are in Christ because of His sacrifice and His desire for us.

2. **What you know matters.** You must recognize that the Word of God is necessary to engage angels. They only heed His voice, which is His Word.

3. **What you practice matters.** You must exercise what you know. Knowledge alone will not do anything for you. *You must pray the Word out loud.* Give the Word of God a voice. His Word being spoken out *in faith* is the same as His voice! Angels will engage with that faith-filled action.

4. **Worship** is a magnet for angelic activity as you see this represented at the throne of God throughout Scripture.

5. **How you live your life is important.** It's not about being good enough; it's about being obedient with what you know to do. If you have a direct word from God for your life, follow it! If you only have the written Word of God as your guide, then follow that with all of your heart. Living a separated life unto the Lord is an act of holiness, and it will attract the forces of Heaven to move on your behalf.

These are guidelines for the rules of engagement. It must be said that God wants you to have Heaven's assistance even more than you want it. It comes through Jesus and a relationship with Him through His Word and the Holy Spirit. That combination alone is irresistible for the forces of Heaven. They will contend for the individual who is in this place. Why? Because of their deep reverence for and commitment to Jesus and because these *servants of fire* were created for this purpose. Lining up your life with a purpose and the assignment God gave you—as well as spending time with the Holy Spirit in worship, prayer, and speaking out God's written Word in faith—will induce effectiveness from angels.

CHAPTER THREE QUESTIONS

1. How do people give the enemy permission to speak into their lives?

_____

_____

_____

_____

_____

_____

2. Have you had a situation in which you called out to God for assistance and the situation changed for you?

_____

_____

_____

_____

_____

_____

3. What are the five rules of engagement listed above and how can you incorporate them into your life?

_____

_____

_____

_____

_____

_____

4. What other Scriptures would you use to boldly speak out in faith for any circumstance you might face?

_____

_____

_____

_____

_____

_____

Chapter Four

THE SECRET *of* VOICE ACTIVATION

The voice of the Lord divides the flames of fire.

Psalm 29:7

S ervants of fire are engaged specifically by the *voice of God*. This matters very much for you. In any given scenario, angels are not moved by you. A person cannot move an angel. They are like police officers with orders—they only answer to headquarters. With a capacity to communicate and express emotion, these angelic beings certainly have a will. It is their will that caused many of them to follow Lucifer in rebellion against God. It is also their will that is most likely the reason the ones who stayed loyal to the Lord during that cosmic insurrection will refuse to break rank or allow even the slightest appearance of disloyalty to God. Consider the angel who was with John in the Book of Revelation. At one point, John fell down to worship the angel and was interrupted by the messenger starkly protesting, "See that you do not do that!"

> *Then he said to me, "Write: 'Blessed are those who are called to the marriage supper of the Lamb!'" And he said to me, "These are the true sayings of God." And I fell at his feet to worship him. But he said to me, "See that you do not*

*do that! I am your fellow servant, and of your brethren
who have the testimony of Jesus. Worship God! For the
testimony of Jesus is the spirit of prophecy."*

—Revelation 19:9-10

Why would this angel respond with such urgency? Almost as
if to say before the Lord, "You see, my Lord, I am nothing like
those wicked angels who rebelled against You! I will have none of
it! Nothing to do with even the slightest appearance or temptation
of being worshiped." When looking at this moment regarding the
angel and John, we must come to the realization that this angel had
not only been loyal to the God of the universe from the beginning,
but *he witnessed the demise and casting out of those who sided with
Lucifer.* He was also keenly aware of what will happen to those who
participated in that angelic uprising. We will go into that in greater
detail in the pages ahead.

By stating, "See that you do not do that!" this *servant of fire*
was rejecting any notion both in the eyes of the Lord and for
himself. When examining this instance, it is safe to assume all
angels who remained with the Lord are more convinced than
ever that they chose wisely. Not only did they know to stand with
the Lord and follow Michael into battle against those renegades,
but they know what happened to so many of their *once brothers*
who violated the purposes of God. Some are in gloomy dungeons, some are bound in geographic locations, and some are still
wandering about, yet will never see the glory of God from the
right side of things ever again. Ultimately, the final destination
of all rebellious angels, no matter their rank or function, will be
the lake of fire. Smoke and torment for all eternity await these
wicked ones.

THE SECRET OF VOICE ACTIVATION

> *Bless the Lord, you His angels, who excel in strength, **who do His word, heeding the voice of His word.** Bless the Lord, all you His hosts, you ministers of His, **who do His pleasure.** Bless the Lord, all His works, in all places of His dominion. Bless the Lord, O my soul!*
> —Psalm 103:20-22

There is a secret that needs to be understood. It might come as a surprise, *but angels don't listen to the voice of man*—they listen to the voice of God! Psalm 29:7 says, "The voice of the Lord divides the flames of fire." This is a reference to angels standing in rank and file; armies of Heaven standing together are suddenly put into order and assigned positions by the voice of God. When God speaks, angels react! In part, this is because it is possible that they were forged right out of God Himself. I only speculate this as one of the designations of God, that He is a consuming fire. Angels are flames of fire. *It could be that angels are simply flames taken straight out of the fire of God.*

Angels don't listen to the voice of man.

In the same way, God made man out of the dirt, and from man came a rib, which was a woman. *This is the precedent for the possibility that the Lord made the angels right out of Himself.* After all, they are magnificent; they are awe-inspiring entities. The heart of God is always one of family. He created angels before He created Adam and Eve. According to Job 38:7, the sons of God were shouting for joy at the creation of all things. Just as everything created by the voice of God responds to His voice, so do the angels. They are created beings, and they respond to His voice and His voice alone. Jesus said He was capable of calling on twelve legions of angels and would have been able to destroy the world many times over. What a tremendous ability. Yet, we must remember, according to His own words, "I AM," Jesus is also the voice of God. Angels will do whatever He says they should do.

Just as everything created by the voice of God responds to His voice, so do the angels.

How does this apply to you? When you speak the written Word of God, angels stand at attention. Angels have a responsibility and are created to respond to His voice. When you speak, declare, pray, worship, or use any other utterance that utilizes the verbalizing of God's written Word spoken through your voice, angels are activated.

ANGELS AND YOUR EMOTIONS

Importantly, it must be known that the *servants of fire* do not respond to *pleading*, they do not respond to *emotions*, nor do they respond to your special *requests* directed at them. Angels are *servants of fire* who are legally engaged by the spoken Word of God. These fiery ones would be denying the very fabric of their creation to defy or deny the voice of God. This might be a difficult thing for many to receive, as they believe it is perfectly natural to "cry out" or even plead with God and even angels to accomplish something they desperately want to see happen. Although this is not the correct way to make your requests known, it is understandable, as people have legitimate emotions and will utilize them when requesting something from the Lord. However, frustration and even great disappointment can be the result of not knowing the proper way to engage the *servants of fire*. Nothing motivates us like results do, and God wants you to experience results even more than you do! We will be dealing with getting the highest results in prayer in greater detail in the pages ahead.

MINISTERING SPIRITS TO THE HEIRS OF SALVATION

Earlier I made the statement that angels only respond to the voice of God. This is true, but there is more to it than God speaking from Heaven and angels hearing His voice and obeying. Angels are moved to *serve the heirs of salvation*. They receive kingdom access and *permission* from believers who speak the Word of God, who have the Word of God in their hearts, and who have the Word of God mixed with their faith. There is compliance with God's way of doing things, which produces covenant empowerment.

When we pray in faith, there isn't necessarily the commanding of angels—they simply know what to do. Meaning, when you take your free moral agency and begin to pray in the Holy Spirit, prayers of faith will engage the authority of God and engage the authority of man, who is a little lower than God according to Psalm 8:5. A combination of man's free moral agency and rank among all created beings offers the authority to pray and authorize angels as well. Again, it should be stated that we are not commanding these fiery servants. Rather, how we pray and the way we engage in warfare prayer brings about kingdom effectiveness.

God's kingdom operates on a set of rules and legal authority that must be exercised in God's way. When we access prayer our way, something good might happen, but it certainly won't be the highest and best use of what the Lord has provided for us. Knowing the Word of God and exercising the power of the Holy Spirit by standing on the written Word of God arms you with the strength required to marshal the forces of Heaven into action.

When praying, I often have a list of scriptures specifically mentioning angels, their assignments, and what they do to please the Lord. I read it out in a legal manner and then pray the prayers of request before the Lord. As a practice, this is not something I do every day, but it is something my family and I utilize for special requests or scenarios requiring specific attention. As in a court of law, there is an effective potency to holding God's Word and promises up to Him. It is a high act of faith. In a court of law, those who know their rights and can recite them, carry a different level of confidence and authority—not in and of themselves, but in what the law says that they can have or not have.

WEAPONIZED AGREEMENT

Utilizing the prayer of agreement is a powerful force. It is what released Peter from prison in Acts. Could it be that the reason we have not seen such profound miracle deliverances is due to brothers and sisters not praying in agreement? It is almost humorous the way the prayer group responded when Peter was actually at their door having been delivered! They scolded Rhoda, the young girl who told them he was there. Their prayers were so effective in agreement that they didn't even believe the outcome or, at the very least, were not expecting the outcome they experienced! Peter was delivered from an impossible scenario!

Agreement was a mighty element when praying for Peter. They were together, which means this prayer group was calling out on behalf of Peter, and it was certainly the right combination to engage an angel. Psalm 91:11-12 says, "For He shall give His angels *charge* over you, to keep you in all your ways. In their hands they *shall bear you up*, lest you dash your foot against a stone." Right there in that jail cell, Peter had both of these things happen to him. Angelic hands were activated, and the charge concerning Peter was in motion.

> *Peter was therefore kept in prison, **but constant prayer was offered to God for him by the church.***
>
> —Acts 12:5

> *And when Herod was about to bring him out, that night Peter was sleeping, bound with two chains between two soldiers; and the guards before the door were keeping the prison. Now behold, an angel of the Lord stood by him, and a light shone in the prison; and **he struck Peter on the side and raised him up**, saying, "Arise quickly!" And his **chains fell off his hands**. Then the angel said*

to him, "Gird yourself and tie on your sandals"; and so he did. And he said to him, "Put on your garment and follow me." So he went out and followed him, and did not know that what was done by the angel was real, but thought he was seeing a vision. When they were past the first and the second guard posts, **they came to the iron gate that leads to the city, which opened to them of its own accord;** *and they went out and went down one street, and immediately the angel departed from him.*

And when Peter had come to himself, he said, "Now I know for certain that the Lord has sent His angel, and has delivered me from the hand of Herod and from all the expectation of the Jewish people." So, when he had considered this, he came to the house of Mary, the mother of John whose surname was Mark, **where many were gathered together praying.**

—Acts 12:6-12

And as Peter knocked at the door of the gate, a girl named Rhoda came to answer. When she recognized Peter's voice, because of her gladness she did not open the gate, but ran in and announced that Peter stood before the gate. But they said to her, "You are beside yourself!" Yet she kept insisting that it was so. So they said, "It is his angel." Now Peter continued knocking; and when they opened the door and saw him, they were astonished.

—Acts 12:13-16

Notice how this angel being activated through prayer (especially the prayer of agreement) was empowered to affect natural things— even objects. So evidently seen in Acts 12 is the physical activity of angels when prayer is involved. Here are the three points of interest we learn from the angel who delivered Peter from custody:

1. The angel specifically struck Peter on the side.

2. This angel apparently caused the chains to fall off Peter's hands.

3. Likely at the hand of this angel, the gates opened of their own accord.

Interestingly, in Acts 16 there is another account of a jail experience involving deliverance. Personally, I am of the persuasion that an angel or angels shook the ground of the prison. Psalm 91:11-12 says, "For He shall *give His angels charge over you, to keep you in all your ways. In their hands* they shall bear you up, lest you dash your foot against a stone." Notice that the angels have charge over us to keep us in all our ways. This references their ability to intervene at any moment when we are walking with the Lord! Specifically, it mentions "their hands." Angels take you up in their hands. Natural scenarios can be touched, moved, or even changed lightly or forcefully by the manipulation of angelic hands. Have you ever wondered how angels can move things? I have, but here we see straight from the Word of God that they do so with their hands! For example, below is another story in the Scriptures telling the account of Paul and Silas' time in prison.

And when they had laid many stripes on them, they threw them into prison, commanding the jailer to keep them *securely. Having received such a charge, **he put them into the inner prison** and fastened their **feet in the stocks**. But at midnight **Paul and Silas were praying and singing** hymns to God, and the prisoners were listening to them. Suddenly **there was a great earthquake**, so that the foundations of the prison were shaken; and immediately **all the doors were opened and everyone's chains were loosed**.*

—Acts 16:23-26

Notice they were in the *inner prison* with their feet fastened in stocks. In response to this gloomy situation, Paul and Silas show us what we ought to be doing in any scenario when things are not going according to the desired outcome—*they prayed and sang!* The inner prison would be like saying they were in solitary confinement with shackles on their feet. Most people would start complaining or even fighting! I'm sure Silas may have thought of saying to Paul, "This is my last trip with you!" or "I didn't know we were called to a jail ministry, Paul!" Nope, that is not how this went. Apostle Paul and prophet Silas began to *pray* to the point of *singing*—two things that activate angels. Much like Peter who had a group in agreement praying for him, these two were in agreement in prayer. Angels were activated with their hands to shake the ground hard enough for shackles to fall off. Not only Paul and Silas, but everyone in the entire prison had their shackles fall off!

It is important who you're around! Prayer and worship are two of the highest ways to voice-activate angels. Specifically, the prayer and praise of agreement!

CHAPTER FOUR QUESTIONS

1. What can you do to activate angels?

   _____

   _____

   _____

   _____

2. What's the difference between emotional prayers and requests versus prayers of faith, declaring the Word of God?

   _____

   _____

   _____

   _____

3. What is the highest and best way to activate the forces of Heaven?

   _____

   _____

   _____

   _____

4. What are two things listed that will activate angels?

_____

_____

_____

_____

5. When faced with a trial, what can you do to activate angels around you to help your situation?

_____

_____

_____

_____

Chapter Five

TALKING *to* STRANGERS *or* ENTERTAINING ANGELS

Do not forget to entertain strangers, for by so doing
some have unwittingly entertained angels.

Hebrews 13:2

I know of many people who have been rescued by or met people who were no longer there after they received a particular message—or simply were encouraged by a person who came out of nowhere. Recently, Heather and I were flying home from a ministry event and found ourselves in the company of a unique lady who seemed to stick with us everywhere we went. *There was something about her.* The way she looked at us and talked with us, even repeating simple phrases I had said earlier before speaking with her. It seemed to us that she was assigned to us on that particular journey. As interesting as it may sound, this experience has happened to me repeatedly.

A TALL MAN

Several years ago, early on in our marriage, Heather and I stopped at a fast-food restaurant in Minneapolis. On the way into the restaurant, I noticed a man sitting on the curb with a cloak on. I ordered food, came back out, and saw that the man was still sitting there. As I got into the car with Heather, we began to drive away. I was overwhelmed with a sense to go back and give that man all the cash that was in my wallet. I fought with it for a moment, as we didn't have much money, and this would be a sacrificial thing to do. Finally, we turned the car around and arrived back at that same restaurant parking lot. The large man was still sitting on the curb. I got out of the car, walked up to him, and handed him everything in my wallet. I said to him, "God bless you, sir, I just wanted to give this to you." He started to laugh, and then he stood up! It was striking how tall he was! He seemed to me as if he was nearly seven feet tall! He looked down at me with powerful eyes and dreadlocks around his shoulders. This large man, with a striking appearance, began to declare over me, "Your Father is so pleased with you! You have done something very pleasing!" He said other declarations that I wish I could remember, but basically he started prophesying to me about the blessings that were to come upon me. It was powerful! He also hugged me nearly off of my feet while laughing!

Now, could this have been a nearly seven-foot-tall, joyful home-less man with well-kept dreadlocks and a large, hooded cloak who also happened to prophesy about my future? Maybe, but there was also a sense in the air—a strong sense of holiness. As we drove away, I remember looking back and not seeing him any longer. It was a powerful experience that Heather and I still talk about some-times. *I personally believe it was an angel.*

HOLDING THE DOOR

Another time I was at a clinic getting my blood drawn for a physical. As this took place, a nurse came into the room where Heather and I were waiting. I was prompted by the Holy Spirit to give her a prophetic word about her life and current relationship, with many other details following. She was about to administer a blood draw, which she did, and the power of God hit her and she began to weep at the same time as she placed a needle in my arm! It was a very uncomfortable Holy Spirit moment! This nurse nearly fell on Heather and me as she explained how she had been crying out to God for direction and if He would please send someone to come talk to her. After this encounter, we were leaving the clinic and an older black man was standing there holding the door for us. It didn't make sense that he had been waiting at the door with it held open for us. I walked past, then paused, stepped back, and looked into this man's eyes. We had just been in a Holy Spirit encounter in the other room, and I sensed the power of God in this situation. I said to him, "Sir, you have very unique eyes, angelic eyes." They had a very bright blue color to them. He smirked at me, and said, "You have a wonderful day." I guess you had to be there, but there was a connection as he looked at me, as if to say, "You got me!" Heather and I both looked at one another and said, "That was an angel watching over our divine assignment!"

PETER'S ANGEL

Dr. Gerald Derstine was a person who was pivotal in starting the charismatic movement back in the 1950s. When I was in my teen years, he took me to minister with him and his wife Beulah. He would tell me stories of his ministry in Israel and the Middle East. One story of interest fascinated me. As I recall it, Dr. Derstine was ministering in a particular meeting when a man approached at the end of the service. The man was adamantly thanking him for coming to see him and his family in a closed Middle Eastern country. The man explained how Dr. Derstine showed up in their living room and began explaining to them that they needed to hear about Jesus and where they should go to hear about Jesus being preached. The man followed the directions and found the place where believers were preaching about Jesus in this closed nation. As a result, he and his entire household became born again! The man was thrilled to see Dr. Derstine again, thanking him for telling them where they could hear the preaching of Jesus in their city. The only thing was, as Dr. Derstine explained, he had never been to the nation mentioned and certainly had never been to this particular city. The man protested saying, "No, you were in our home! You explained to us where to go in detail! Thank you!" Dr. Derstine didn't know how to respond. Later, after thinking about it, the Holy Spirit led him to the account of Peter when he was released from prison.

> *And as Peter knocked at the door of the gate, a girl named Rhoda came to answer. When she recognized Peter's voice, because of her gladness she did not open the gate, but ran in and announced that Peter stood before the gate. But they said to her, "You are beside yourself!" Yet she kept insisting that it was so. So they said, "**It is his angel.**"*
>
> —Acts 12:13-15

What a fascinating passage, leading up to a remarkable statement! Dr. Derstine was convinced that he experienced what these believers declared to the servant girl, Rhoda, in the Book of Acts: "It is his angel." He was convinced that this was what happened to him—that his angel appeared to that family and told them how to find where the gospel was being preached. It is an interesting point that angels do not preach the gospel, but they can point people where to go. What a powerful story.

HEATHER SPOKE TO AN ANGEL

There was an experience that Heather had when she was seventeen years old. She was shopping at a store and a tall, blonde-haired lady came up to her. Throughout her time in the store, she kept running into this woman. Heather noticed that every time she ran into her, her basket was empty. As Heather came outside, there was a commotion outside the doors, with bad characters. As Heather walked outside, she stood at the curb to enter the parking lot, waiting for her mom to pick her up. Suddenly, the tall, blonde-haired woman was standing next to her. Heather again noticed that she didn't have any bags with her from the store. The woman looked down at Heather, and for a moment she stood right next to her, nearly touching Heather. The woman then looked up and straight ahead. Heather looked away and saw her mom pulling up with the car and she looked back to say goodbye to the woman standing there. The moment she looked back, the woman was gone! Amazingly enough, they were standing at the end of an open parking lot and there was literally nowhere for her to have gone. Heather said to her mom when she pulled up, "Did you see that woman?" her mom replied, "No, what woman?" Heather felt such a sense of peace when this woman was by her. It was likely for protection. She was most likely an angel.

A Holy Roar

One encounter that stands out mightily in my mind is from a moment that took place during a conference in Minneapolis. I was leading worship with several musicians and singers. As we stepped into a place of praise, it elevated to a place of prophetic music and then erupted into a spontaneous song! It came in wave after wave of song and proclamation. What started out as prophesying and spontaneous singing continued ascending until a holy shout began to fill the room! First by the people in attendance, then by the singers and even musicians. A shout that seemed to continue for quite some time! At the height of this moment, the shout grew into what I can only describe as *a roar*. The volume became bigger than the space we were in! Volume and Holy Spirit power were present and even became palpable as this roar grew. Suddenly, the roar was beyond what we could generate in the ballroom we were meeting in! It's as if to say we started the roar, but others joined in to finish it! Volume escalated, our shouting rose, and for a moment it seemed as if it was suspended in time. There was a stadium-sized roar in that ballroom. It was *not human*—it was beyond any of us and well beyond the possibility of a manufactured shout. Whether we were brought into the spirit realm or the spirit realm invaded us, there was a holy reverence that I carried all the way out of that service. One of my team members looked at me later that night and said, "What happened? Were those angels shouting with us?" What marked it so powerfully was the presence of God at that moment. Not only was there an unbelievable roar from Heaven in the room, but it was marked by an intense presence of holiness.

SPECIAL MESSAGE FROM THE THRONE OF GOD

One of the reasons I chose to write this book is due to the most notable time I've directly encountered an angelic messenger. It was the time Heather and I were doing a live broadcast from our home. After finishing the broadcast, there was a strong presence of the Holy Spirit resting upon us. She was sitting on the stairway near the living room, while I was sitting with my back to a wall and a window directly behind me. As this moment began to increase with intensity, I began to weep from the sense of power filling the room. Our setting changed. An environment of peace and stillness turned into a spiritually charged atmosphere; holiness and reverence were mightily in the room—and *increasing with intensity!* I looked over to Heather with tears now streaming down my face and said, "Something is happening!"

As the power of God continued filling the space, there was a point I almost began to shout and cry due to the intensity in the room. When suddenly a voice spoke from behind me with power, saying, "I come to you from the throne of God and carry a message! There is coming a turn of the tide, and the great God of Heaven has more need of you after the 2020 election than He does now at this time. *Prepare!* There will be a new team, and new ways." Among many details that this angelic messenger said to me, there were particular events regarding my family and how I was to go forward regarding them. Additionally, this messenger spoke directly to me about a specific assignment that had been sent to destroy us and that the Lord would deliver us from it. It turned out to be exactly what the messenger had said and played out how we were told.

There were many things said, and that particular encounter even engaged the gift of prophecy that works in my life. Prophecy burst out of me at that moment regarding things that would come. The intense presence of God will do that. It was monumental and powerful for us to the point I was so overwhelmed, it seemed as though I was going to collapse or scream. Many more details were shared with us that day and it was very encouraging with clear direction for us.

MESSENGERS AT UNIQUE MOMENTS AND OCCASIONS

Over the years, I have personally encountered a variety of messengers who walked up to me in public. They have given me messages and spoken prophetic declarations to me. These types of scenarios may simply be people on assignment to tell me something, or they very well could have been angelic messengers. One time a man walked up to me with an African accent. I was at a social event in the basement of a small church. I was thinking about fading away from public ministry and empowering everyone else I was raising up at the time to run with the ball. This man walked up to me and said, "I have a message for you. You cannot quit now, the books must be written, and the message must go out!" This man walked away from me. He was not a part of the church, not a part of the gathering, no one knew who he was, and I had never seen him before or since. His word was right on and encouraged me to continue!

RESCUED AT A PARTY

A lady Heather and I know very well was telling the story to us of a time when she was at a party. Then all of a sudden, she felt "off" and realized she most likely had been drugged. Her senses were dulling when two men walked up, one on each side of her, grabbing her arms and forcefully pushing her to the exit door. She said she was afraid but was unable to fight back or stop this from happening. As they opened the door, a man walked in and stepped in front of this scenario saying, "You can't leave! I've been looking for you." Now, this woman did not know the man and had never seen him before. He looked at the two men forcing her out the door and they ran off. The man had a beard and was very kind. She said to the man who rescued her, "You look like Jesus!" to which he replied, "Maybe that's where I am from." Then he was gone.

Angels seem to come as messengers during pivotal moments or to announce things as they change. This was the case with the shepherds seeing angels proclaiming. Think about the time an announcement came to Mary that she would have a child. Over and over again this scenario is the way the Lord has chosen to announce things to His people from generations past and still today.

I once was in prayer and saw an angel named Red, White, and Blue. This angel wanted to stand but was standing alone. I saw a white and blue angel not far off, and if these two would remain together, neither would fall. I know these two angels represented the nations of America and Israel. When this assignment is violated, much like any nation not treating Israel properly, it's as if protection will lift, and terrible events are able to manifest.

Countless Bible stories tell of angels bearing news, making declarations, fighting battles, delivering prisoners, and so much more. The Lord desires for us to have the right relationship with angelic messengers and servants.

Below is a list of scriptures showing the majority of encounters people have had in the Bible with angels. Scripture records at least 100 or more interactions between angelic messengers and humans.

1. **Hagar**—Genesis 16:7-11; Genesis 21:17

2. **Abraham**—Genesis 18:2; Genesis 22:11; Genesis 22:15

3. **Lot and Sodomites**—Genesis 19:1-22

4. **Jacob**—Genesis 28:12; Genesis 31:11; Genesis 32:1

5. **Moses**—Exodus 3:2

6. **Balaam**—Numbers 22:22-35

7. **Joshua**—Hebrews 5:1-14:15; Exodus 23:20-23; Exodus 32:34

8. **Israel**—Judges 2:1-5

9. **Gideon**—Judges 6:11-22

10. **Manoah and his wife**—Judges 13:9-21

11. **David**—2 Samuel 24:1-25; 1 Chronicles 21:1-30

12. **Elijah**—1 Kings 19:5-7; 2 Kings 1:3; 2 Kings 1:15

13. **Elisha and his Servant**—2 Kings 6:16-17

14. **Assyrians**—2 Kings 19:35; Isaiah 37:36

15. **Hebrew children**—Daniel 3:25-28

16. **Nebuchadnezzar**—Daniel 3:24-25

17. **Daniel**—Hebrews 6:1-20:22; Daniel 8:16; Daniel 9:21; Daniel 10:5-21; Daniel 12:5-7

18. **Zechariah**—Hebrews 1:8-19; Zechariah 2:3; Zechariah 3:1-6; Zechariah 4:1-5; Zechariah 5:5-10; Zechariah 6:4-5; Zechariah 12:8

19. **Joseph**—Matthew 1:20; Matthew 2:13; Matthew 2:19

20. **Mary**—Luke 1:26-38

21. **Zacharias**—Luke 1:20-38

22. **Shepherds**—Luke 2:9-14

23. **Jesus**—Matthew 4:11; Luke 22:43

24. **Mary Magdalene**—Matthew 28:1-5

25. **The Disciples**—Acts 1:11

26. **Peter and John**—Acts 5:19

27. **Philip**—Acts 8:26

28. **Cornelius**—Acts 10:3; Acts 10:30-32

29. **Peter**—Acts 12:7-11

30. **Paul**—Acts 27:23

31. **John**—Over 50 angelic encounters in the Book of Revelation

CHAPTER FIVE QUESTIONS

1. Have you ever met someone you thought was or could have been an angel?

   _____

2. If so, what was the situation and how did you come to the conclusion that it was an angel?

   _____
   _____
   _____
   _____
   _____

3. Hebrews 13:2: "Do not forget to entertain strangers, for by so doing some have unwittingly entertained angels." What are ways that you can put this scripture into practice?

   _____
   _____
   _____
   _____
   _____

Chapter Six

MESSENGERS *of* DECEPTION

And no wonder! For Satan himself transforms
himself into an angel of light.

2 Corinthians 11:14

I n the previous chapter, we looked at faith-filled angelic encounters. Yet, something of deep concern is the growing *infatuation*
with the supernatural, particularly in the area where angels are
concerned. Now, please understand, there is nothing wrong with
desiring the supernatural as it relates to God and the Holy Spirit.
First Corinthians 14 even exhorts us to "desire spiritual gifts," which
is absolutely supernatural. Many of our encounters with Jesus are
filled with supernatural moments. It is, however, the infatuation
with the supernatural minus a deep love of the truth that allows
deception to position itself right around the corner.

You see, experiences are wonderful when they involve the supernatural movement of the Holy Spirit. My life has been forever
impacted as a result of dramatic supernatural encounters, which I
thank God for, and I expect to experience many more Holy Spirit
moments. What is of great concern is the way many people place
experiences (or the deep desire for them) in such a high regard
that it leads to irresponsibility. An encounter alone should not be
the verification for any scenario when it comes to supernatural

events—especially in the arena of *angelic visitations.* Stories are accelerating every day related to angelic scenarios and visitations. Again, I personally believe in angelic visitations and definitely welcome every God-sent messenger that the Lord would deem necessary for me to encounter. It's thrilling when this type of thing happens. What is of utmost importance is discernment.

Please listen to me carefully, as it is vital for the days we are living in. More than ever, there is a mania related to these things. The concerning issue comes down to more than just false experiences. Certain individuals may sensationalize an encounter for attention. This is a very unhealthy thing that can happen. The listener believes the sensationalized story that was never true. Damage ensues as it leads the listener to have false expectations based on smoke, mirrors, and storytelling.

For all encounters, it is of utmost importance that we do not sensationalize things, as it can lead to deception. One of the most tragic forms of deception is *self-deception.* Someone might ask, "Why is that so tragic?" Well, it is self-deception that takes shape in a person's life when they are not honest with themselves about experiences or their encounters. If a person embellishes the truth and they know they are doing so, it will eventually lead to self-deception and ruin their own heart's confidence in themselves.

It is highly important that we tell the truth of a matter for the sake of our own hearts so we have inner integrity. Self-deception lays a foundation that is very unhealthy to build on. Beyond this is the issue of outside deception. Supernatural forces are always looking for avenues to enter through. The first step is bending the truth, then doing it again and again until ultimately a violation of the gospel can take place.

We notice that when referencing the authority of the gospel he was preaching, Paul refers to two points. In Galatians 1:8, he states, "if *we*, or an *angel* from heaven." His statement in this Scripture goes in line with 2 Corinthians 11:13, where Paul again warns his listeners about false teachers and false ministers operating by cloaking themselves as legitimate ministers.

> *But even if we, or an angel from heaven, preach any other gospel to you than what we have preached to you, let him be accursed.*
>
> —Galatians 1:8

> *For such are false apostles, deceitful workers, transforming themselves into apostles of Christ.*
>
> —2 Corinthians 11:13

It is fascinating to take into consideration that Paul speaks of false fivefold ministers and angels in the *same context*. Often, this Scripture has given me pause when dealing with the realm of the supernatural. Now, for those who are mature, having their senses exercised to discern both good and evil, this is not really a problem. Even true angels would always direct all glory straight to the Lord Jesus Christ. For example, the angel in Revelation 19:10, who saw that John was falling down to worship him, said to John, "See that you do not do that!" and "Worship God!" going on to say, "The testimony of Jesus is the spirit of prophecy." This is how *legitimate* angelic encounters go according to Scripture. They always point to God the Father, Jesus the Son, or simply are present to execute the wishes of the Godhead. A growing area of concern, especially in prophetic circles, is many runaway notions regarding angelic interactions. Very seldom do these encounters have a scriptural basis, nor does anyone care to question the validity of these moments. Many of these could very well be legitimate, but regardless, we must hold fast to the Word of God when considering the narratives of those who have frequent encounters with such entities.

DECEPTION

*For false christs and false prophets will rise and show great
signs and wonders to deceive, if possible, even the elect.*

—Matthew 24:24

Could it be, if possible, that in the last days even the elect would be deceived? We read that there will be false christs and false prophets equipped and ready to deceive the masses. Not only will these arise, but the enemy will also use people to share things that didn't really happen. To stretch the truth, so to say. Those who aren't in tune with the Holy Spirit and the Word of God could possibly be deceived. *It is so important for every believer to test the spirits!* It can be highly offensive to someone having an experience or an encounter to then be questioned about its authenticity. There are those who will *believe anything they experience, fabricate an encounter,* or *even worse*—intentionally *create narratives* for the purpose of deception. Sadly, some will intentionally deceive others by fabricating an encounter and using people's gullibility for their own agenda. Tragically, there are those who believe them and hold them as truth.

An error is a symptom of not keeping the Word of God as the main point of reference.

Without examining what we hear under the scope of the Bible, deception is being fostered. Please know, just because an angelic encounter might take place in your life, or someone tells you about their encounter, that doesn't mean it's trustworthy. If the angel comes glorifying Jesus Christ and confirming the Word of God, then all is well, but it is more important than ever to be sure whatever you are experiencing is not outside of biblical scope.

Sometimes, when speaking with people about their encounters, I am led to the conclusion that they have intellectually rationalized what they have experienced or testified to. Their encounter or experience is, in all reality, an imagination they have chosen to embrace as some kind of revelatory experience. Dangerous ground begins to be walked on when these types of things are as easy to experience as having a thought.

> *That you may learn in us not to think beyond what is written, that none of you may be puffed up on behalf of one against the other.*
> **—1 Corinthians 4:6**

ANGEL OF LIGHT

The angel of light is deception at its finest. If you are gullible to encounters that are off, but only *mildly*, then falsehood can creep in until full-blown deception takes hold. An angel of light might have little trouble deceiving such individuals pre-filled with this type of self-deception. These are the sort who, upon any encounter, are wildly blown away, having little foundation to bring balance. These easily surrender to deceptive persuasions.

What does an angel of light want?
The answer is access.

Angels of light appear for permission. For the non-discerning, they would be just another angelic messenger, beautiful and arrayed in glorious splendor. After all, *mankind is not used to seeing into the spirit realm,* so even the lowest level manifestation could rock the non-discerning into compliance and willingness to cooperate.

BATTLE FOR ALLEGIANCE

Here is an example from my life as a very young boy. When I was nine years old, there was a *battle for my allegiance.* It's hard to describe it any other way. Ever since I was very young, hearing God and experiencing supernatural things was a frequent occurrence in my life.

One particular day, I was in a field on the ranch I grew up on. This was a regular occurrence for me, to be out in the fields and near the woods on our large property. Often my afternoons would be spent walking by the large river, which bordered the land. It was a very pleasant and enjoyable thing for me to do as a young person. However, there was something that began to happen. At first, it was infrequent but grew into a regular occasion. It was the audible sound of a voice. A clear and direct voice, similar to an echo, but more intentional. It would shout my name over the trees; it sounded and felt as if it was in the wind. Day after day this experience would happen to me when out on those far-back acres. In response, I would rush home on an ATV, fully believing my father was calling me from a long distance. After asking him a few times what he wanted, he would respond that he didn't call me. I relegated it to an unknown source as I had no way of identifying the cause or origin of such a phenomenon.

Today, however, I know it was God calling me when I was young, much like the prophet Samuel. Yet, there was another side to this experience. A little more of a scary encounter also took place. One day, a different voice called to me as well. It started out similar to the voice calling me over the trees. Only this one was intense, darker, and felt scary. The sensation that came along with it was sinister and invasive. It got closer each time it called me until, finally, I sensed it was right next to me, only to confirm my intuition by speaking audibly. "Joe," it said. At this moment, my courageous German shepherd bristled and growled in the direction of the voice, then, to my surprise, whimpered with his ears dropping back, and he ran away! Not something I expected to see! The combination of my dog running away, mixed with the voice I just heard right by me, caused me terror so I jumped onto my ATV and drove away as quickly as I could!

When in doubt, cast it out!

It wasn't until later, after receiving Jesus as my Savior, that I began to understand what had happened. Both light and darkness recognized the gifts in my life, and each side was attempting to speak to me. This can be a factor for certain people based on the type of spiritual gift they may carry from birth. *Especially prophetic people,* who can have a gift in operation in their lives even before they receive Jesus as Lord. Sadly, much like a person who has a gift to sing—who can either use it for the world or use it in a church—spiritual gifts can be similar. Let me explain. Encounters with spiritual forces can lead to the wrong conclusion without having a relationship with Jesus. Those who don't understand how gifting works (and who is the author of such gifts) may begin to dabble in dark things such as psychic activity, believing the gift they possess is for clairvoyance and various forms of witchcraft. Nothing could be further from the truth, as God is the author of every good and perfect gift. It is an agenda of darkness to pervert these wonderful gifts given by God.

A true conversion with Jesus Christ is the real answer for navigating the gifts in anyone's life. Once a person gives their life to Jesus, what must take place is a dedication to the written Word of God. God's Word is the plumb line that rightsizes experiences. It definitely taught me the meaning of the famous saying, "When in doubt, cast it out!"

Now, I bring this issue to light because many people not rooted in the Word of God play along with strange encounters. Some entities may come across as not evil at all. They may be presented in an interesting, intriguing, or even kind way. I found that the answer to any experience is to not go beyond what is written and you will never go astray. What these voices were competing over was me. I go into this type of understanding in-depth when I teach the *School of the Prophets* or do prophetic training. These two voices—one being the Holy Spirit, the other a demonic force—were both calling me. One was to enter into the prophetic calling God had ordained for me; the other was a psychic spirit wanting me to give it access to a variety of evil. This type of scenario is a gateway to talking to what many believe are spirits of the departed and many other evil tricks the Devil uses for access by permission. Darkness needs cooperation from people, especially those who are more sensitive to the spiritual realm. When individuals engage in any supernatural experiences that are not of God and His Word, they are giving access via permission to enter their lives!

> *Do not forget to entertain strangers, for by so doing some have unwittingly entertained angels.*
>
> **—Hebrews 13:2**

Be aware that you may be entertaining angels. "Entertaining angels" has always been a scripture that made me think of times angels may stand before you in the form of a person. Yet, please also consider this thought. Fallen angels may also have the ability to appear as a person or manifest in the form of any other type of entity.

Permission to Manifest

Could it be that fallen angels have the ability to appear? This could be the cause of such phenomena as UFOs—what some would consider alien entities—and the encounters many have talked about. What if many of the paranormal issues that seem to be rising are simply "angels of light" that are exercising their ability to manifest into the natural world in a variety of shapes and bodily forms?

How are they empowered to manifest? The answer is similar to the angels of God. God's angels, *the servants of fire*, manifest by the voice of God and in a place where the kingdom of God is being enforced through human beings. The same is true on the opposite side of humanity wherever there is a compromise, evil, fear, false beliefs, or anything else that goes contrary to the Word of God and His kingdom system. Proverbs 29:2 says, "When a wicked man rules, the people groan." However, Proverbs 14:34 says, "Righteousness exalts a nation, but sin is a reproach to any people." Additionally, Matthew 18:18 says, "Assuredly, I say to you, whatever you bind on earth will be bound in heaven, and whatever you loose on earth will be loosed in heaven." Think about how horrible it must have been in cultures in which human sacrifice was normal. Evil was celebrated and, in a way, even legislated! This type of culture would arguably empower fallen angel activity through human permission, allowing access to the natural world.

Through their nefarious deceptions, demonic entities are granted much more latitude to do what they desire when a culture allows it corporately. This is why we must be alert and watch for our enemy, the Devil, who prowls around like a roaring lion seeking whom he may devour (see 1 Peter 5:8). He seeks whom he may devour by putting his voice out in front of unwitting individuals.

Those who take on his persuasion begin acting out on what he suggests. This happens in thoughts, emotions, and the human experience. If this persists, permission is granted by cooperation with those thoughts or fiery darts of the enemy. Cooperation means permission and access are granted. A host of evil actions can manifest greatly by this type of access, which includes demonic, fallen angel manifestations. Society is falling deeper and deeper into deception, being fixated on darkness and evil and embracing a variety of wickedness. The result of this is we see more reports of strange things in the sky, unusual paranormal encounters, and even a heightened volume of angel experiences. One of many reasons that we are to resist the Devil through the Word of God is to avoid encounters with angels of light!

SEEING ANGELS FREQUENTLY

There is nothing in the Word of God telling us it is wrong to see angels or even to see them frequently. A warning does come, however, when there is a fixation with them leading to a type of worship. *Severe warnings* seem to be tied to mankind and angelic interactions when it is from a place of people *looking for angels* or even *worshiping them.*

> *Let no one cheat you of your reward, taking delight in false humility and worship of angels, intruding into those things which he has not seen, vainly puffed up by his fleshly mind.*
>
> **—Colossians 2:18**

115

It needs to be said again that access comes through the forces of permission. To gain permission, there must be a request made, and the number-one way a request is made by darkness is through *persuasion* and *deception*. *Angels of light* may be better labeled as *angels of deception*. Anyone should be very cautious when venturing into things they have not seen. Why? Because stories and testimonies are very subjective; they can be fabricated, even purposefully crafted to deceive. But even more critical is the high potential of encountering something or deceiving your own heart to the point that deep deception takes root. This is the desire of evil entities, demons, or fallen angels. Let's look at the following scripture from 2 Peter.

CLOUDS WITHOUT WATER, ETC.

*These are wells without water, clouds carried by a tempest, for whom is reserved the blackness of darkness forever. For when **they speak great swelling words of emptiness, they allure through the lusts of the flesh, through lewdness, the ones who have actually escaped from those who live in error.** While **they promise them liberty**, they themselves are slaves of corruption; for by whom a person is overcome, by him also he is brought into bondage.*

—2 Peter 2:17-19

This is a fascinating scripture as it gives insight into the heart of deception and the deceivers.

These are wells without water.

They are clouds carried by a tempest.

They speak great swelling words of emptiness.

They allure through the lusts of the flesh.

Notice whom they draw away or allure. The word *allure* is the Greek word *deleázō* meaning "to bait, entrap." Notice how deception regarding spiritual encounters begins as "wells without water, clouds carried by a tempest" and goes into the speech of "great swelling words of emptiness." This leads to the allure or bait and entrapment.

The progression goes as follows: *wells with no water* or the image of places that are supposed to quench thirst but are empty. *Clouds carried by a tempest* are a storm with no rain, yet lots of show. Next comes *great swelling words*, or amazing stories and testimonies that are mind-blowing! Finally, this progression of deception even takes away the purity of those who have escaped from those who live in error. How do they lose their purity? Through the *temptation of lewdness*.

Deceivers who tell tall tales of supernatural encounters or bait believers through the lust of the flesh, Scripture points out, are those who have once already escaped these types of people only to be captured again by their tall tales and lust of the flesh. They become captivated through lewdness or lasciviousness, and in every indulgence a person can be entangled. It's as if these liars telling their stories (that they have not truly ventured into) are so self-deceived that they develop a deep-rooted perversion that becomes a stumbling block and temptation for previously delivered believers.

Angels of light work exactly the same way but come in a variety of deceptive ways, ranging from knowledge or dabbling in things that should not be dabbled in, such as narcotics, hallucinogens, or sexual unions. In the case of the believing supernatural crowd, it starts off with just a little bit of storytelling. *Tall tales grow more and more outlandish until the hearers compromise their discernment.* After refusing to check what is being stated, individuals eventually allow their hearts to become hardened. A symptom of a hardened heart is the susceptibility to higher forms of evil, which ultimately leads to gross perversion. By the way, this is where nearly every cult ends up—gross perversion. It all begins with not loving the truth, or a better way of saying it would be, they quit loving the Word of God and all it says.

We must check our supernatural experiences and certainly consider the discernment God gave us when we hear others' stories.

> *But solid food belongs to those who are of full age, that is, those who by reason of use have their senses exercised to discern both good and evil.*
>
> —Hebrews 5:14

When Hebrews references "those who have their senses exercised to discern both good and evil," it is speaking of your *five senses.* Meaning, we are to take our five senses and train them by the written Word of God! That's correct—you read that right. What you can see, smell, taste, touch, and feel must be under subjection to the Word of God. Safety will be the result for any believer who surrenders their natural impulses to the Word of God. This is very beneficial for spiritual encounters and discerning the encounters of others. A shield is also in place against the perversion that often accompanies spiritual deception.

LOVERS OF THE TRUTH

When mankind ventures into realms they are not permitted by God to go into, it is rebellion; additionally, it is a place of great deception. If any person or believer accesses the realm of the spirit outside of what God has authorized, they are open to spiritual deception. If a person believes something from the realm of the spirit that is not authorized by God, they have empowered deception. This is part of the concern I have regarding the angel of light.

Let's look at these scriptures that refer to the Devil disguising himself as an angel of light.

> *But I fear, lest somehow, as the serpent deceived Eve by his craftiness, so your minds may be corrupted from the simplicity that is in Christ. For if he who comes preaches another Jesus whom we have not preached, or if you receive a different spirit which you have not received, or a different gospel which you have not accepted—you may well put up with it! For I consider that I am not at all inferior to the most eminent apostles. Even though I am untrained in speech, yet I am not in knowledge. But we have been thoroughly manifested among you in all things. Did I commit sin in humbling myself that you might be exalted, because I preached the gospel of God to you free of charge? I robbed other churches, taking wages from them to minister to you. And when I was present with you, and in need, I was a burden to no one, for what I lacked the brethren who came from Macedonia supplied. And in everything I kept myself from being burdensome to you, and so I will keep myself. As the truth of Christ is in me, no one shall stop me*

from this boasting in the regions of Achaia. Why? Because I do not love you? God knows! But what I do, I will also continue to do, **that I may cut off the opportunity from those who desire an opportunity to be regarded just as we are in the things of which they boast.** *For such are* **false apostles, deceitful workers, transforming themselves into apostles of Christ.** *And no wonder! For* **Satan himself transforms himself into an angel of light.** *There-fore it is no great thing if his ministers also transform themselves into ministers of righteousness,* *whose end will be according to their works.*

—2 Corinthians 11:3-15

MASTER OF DISGUISE

When looking at the above passage, we see the word *transform*. The Greek word for *transform* is *metaschēmatízō*. It means "to *give* a certain *form* to something, *to change in fashion* or *appearance.*" *It carries the idea of a disguise.* In context, this means that the Devil and his workers will attempt to *mimic* or *disguise* themselves as workers of God. Second Corinthians 11:3-15 shows us that angels of light and false apostles have one thing in common. They transform or *disguise themselves* for the purpose of deception. Again, we ask the question, "Why the deception?" The answer is to gain permission. Both God and the Devil are territorial, and whoever gets permission is the one who gains the territory.

An example from early extra-biblical Jewish tradition tells the story of how the Devil *disguised* himself to influence Job's wife as an angel or in other ways. Some texts suggest he turned himself into a beautiful woman; others say as a beggar. The point is all throughout history the Devil has been seen as one who is capable of disguise. Today, his only weapon against the believer is deception and influence until an embracing of what is being introduced takes place. Discernment comes from time in the Word of God, prayer, and exercising the five senses for the service of God's Word. Dealing with deception is simple.

"The best way to show that a stick is crooked is not to argue about it or to spend time denouncing it, but to lay a straight stick alongside it." —D.L. Moody

---

A requirement, for every believer, is to discover the truth and to love the truth. Deception has a great influence on those who would prefer a story rather than the truth. It is the truth we know and exercise that sets us free!

> *And you shall know the truth, and the truth shall make you free.*
>
> —John 8:32

Knowing the truth keeps you free of the Devil's devices. God's truth and loving the truth will keep you free.

> *Lest Satan should take advantage of us; for we are not ignorant of his **devices**.*
>
> —2 Corinthians 2:11

The word *devices* could be interpreted from the Greek as "mind games." The Devil wants to get you involved in mind games, confusion, and his influence.

REBELLION AS WITCHCRAFT

A certain element that goes along with deception is the issue of rebellion. Now, this is very prevalent in today's society. Rebellion is encouraged and taught as a good thing. It is just the opposite. The term *rebellion* is as the sin of witchcraft, as sometimes stated, but it may not be fully understood. Let's take a brief look into the Scripture reference below and look at what this means in greater depth.

> *So Samuel said: "Has the Lord as great delight in burnt offerings and sacrifices, as in obeying the voice of the Lord? Behold, to obey is better than sacrifice, and to heed than the fat of rams. For **rebellion is as the sin of witchcraft**, and stubbornness is as iniquity and idolatry. Because you have rejected the word of the Lord, He also has rejected you from being king."*
>
> —1 Samuel 15:22-23

When taking the above Scripture in context, we are able to ascertain a definition for the phrase, "Rebellion is as the sin of witchcraft." First of all, we need to recognize that rebellion is a violation of authority. In the case of Saul and Samuel, it was a violation of God's authority. But how is this tied together with witchcraft? The answer is man's will over God's will. When a man decides he will place his own desires or actions above what God has instructed him to do, this is an act of rebellion.

When it comes to spiritual things, acts of rebellion are defined by a person who wants to access the realm of the spirit by their own means. Behavior such as this is tragic. Samuel called out to Saul regarding what he saw inside Saul's character. Saul attempted to play it off; however, God was not pleased. Later on, we see Saul actually stepped into witchcraft by engaging with the witch of En Dor to pull Samuel up from the grave. When Samuel was pulled up, it really was him. He was in paradise, or Abraham's bosom, for Jesus had not yet led the captives and the saints of old out of that place and into Heaven. This action, by Saul, was the fulfillment of what he started when he disobeyed Samuel's words, "To obey is better than sacrifice." Below is the account of Saul's encounter with the witch of En Dor.

WITCH OF EN DOR

*Now **Samuel had died**, and all Israel had lamented for him and buried him in Ramah, in his own city. And Saul had put the mediums and the spiritists out of the land. Then the Philistines gathered together, and came and encamped at Shunem. So Saul gathered all Israel together, and they encamped at Gilboa. **When Saul saw the army of the Philistines, he was afraid, and his heart trembled*** *greatly. And when Saul inquired of the Lord, the Lord did not answer him, either by dreams or by Urim or by the prophets.*

Then Saul said to his servants, "Find me a woman who is a medium, that I may go to her and inquire of her."

And his servants said to him, "In fact, there is a woman who is a medium at En Dor."

So Saul disguised himself and put on other clothes, and he went, and two men with him; and they came to the woman by night. And he said, **"Please conduct a séance for me, and bring up for me the one I shall name to you."**

Then the woman said to him, "Look, you know what Saul has done, how he has cut off the mediums and the spiritists from the land. Why then do you lay a snare for my life, to cause me to die?"

And Saul swore to her by the Lord, saying, "As the Lord lives, no punishment shall come upon you for this thing." Then the woman said, "Whom shall I bring up for you?" And he said, "Bring up Samuel for me." **When the woman saw Samuel, she cried out with a loud voice. And the woman spoke to Saul, saying, "Why have you deceived me? For you are Saul!"** And the king said to her, "Do not be afraid. What did you see?"

And the woman said to Saul, "I saw a spirit ascending out of the earth." So he said to her, "What is his form?" And she said, "An old man is coming up, and he is covered with a mantle." And Saul perceived that it was Samuel, and he stooped with his face to the ground and bowed down.

Now Samuel said to Saul, "Why have you disturbed me by bringing me up?"

And Saul answered, "I am deeply distressed; for the Philistines make war against me, and God has departed from me and does not answer me anymore, neither by prophets nor by dreams. Therefore I have called you, that you may reveal to me what I should do."

Then Samuel said: "So why do you ask me, seeing the Lord has departed from you and has become your enemy? And the Lord has done for Himself as He spoke by me. For the Lord has torn the kingdom out of your hand and given it to your neighbor, David. Because you did not obey the voice of the Lord nor execute His fierce wrath upon Amalek, therefore the Lord has done this thing to you this day. Moreover the Lord will also deliver Israel with you into the hand of the Philistines. And tomorrow you and your sons will be with me. The Lord will also deliver the army of Israel into the hand of the Philistines."

Immediately Saul fell full length on the ground, and was dreadfully afraid because of the words of Samuel. And there was no strength in him, for he had eaten no food all day or all night.

And the woman came to Saul and saw that he was severely troubled, and said to him, "Look, your maidservant has obeyed your voice, and I have put my life in my hands and heeded the words which you spoke to me."

—1 Samuel 28:3-21

Saul had gone from disobeying Samuel to fully exercising witchcraft!

125

WITCHCRAFT IS AN UNAUTHORIZED
USE OF SUPERNATURAL POWER

We can see a glaring example of rebellion and witchcraft going hand in hand through the story of the Tower of Babel. Nimrod was a ruler and built a city in the Valley of Shinar. One of the most infamous structures in all of history was fashioned in this location—the Tower of Babel, a tower to reach the heavens.

> *And they said, "Come, let us build ourselves a city, and a tower whose top is in the heavens; let us make a name for ourselves, lest we be scattered abroad over the face of the whole earth."*
>
> *But the Lord came down to see the city and the tower which the sons of men had built. And the Lord said, "Indeed the people are one and they all have one language, and this is what they begin to do; now nothing that they propose to do will be withheld from them."*
>
> **—Genesis 11:4-6**

Here is the remarkable part regarding the Tower of Babel. Not only was this a *wonder* of the world at the time, but some accounts suggest it was a high tower well into the sky, while others suggest it may have been more of a ceremonial structure. As a ceremonial structure, it might have been a *ziggurat*, much like the Mayans and Aztecs utilized for their worship of deities. What this story is really talking about is a tower that was built to reach another dimension. Nimrod and his followers were looking to access the realm of the spirit without the permission of God. This is why God had to come down and strike the language. The Lord wasn't concerned about mankind building a tower up into the sky and the heavens; rather, this was a tower to access the realms of the spirit or supernatural without God's permission.

An interesting point is found in the name of Nimrod. His name means "we rebel," and that is what these people came together to do—rebel. In this case, it was through unauthorized access to the realm of the spirit. They wanted to encounter all things supernatural, only without God. This may have much to do with all the nefarious issues that took place in Genesis 6, regarding angels who stepped down and co-mingled with the daughters of men. As you will see in the chapters ahead, fallen angels, or watchers, came down and gave humanity all kinds of secrets they were not meant to have. This Tower of Babel was likely part of their evil agenda. The watchers or angels with a wicked agenda also needed permission from mankind to access the natural realm fully. This could very well be the reason behind the tower being built. Could it have been a gateway for angelic wickedness to step into the natural world with human permission? As speculative as that sounds, something was taking place that was serious enough for God to intervene.

Witchcraft is unauthorized access to the realm of the spirit. Both those who do not obey authority in the natural and those who disobey on a spiritual level are the same. Both are unauthorized violations of authority.

> But even if we, or **an angel from heaven**, preach any other gospel to you than what we have preached to you, let him be accursed.
>
> —Galatians 1:8

There are a few things that could be taking place regarding those who claim things they likely have not truly seen or experienced.

1. **Fake encounters**: Simply experiences that are contrived by the imagination of misguided people desiring the experience more than the truth.

2. **Self-deception**: As unique as it may sound, through my experiences with the prophetic I have seen such a need for people to be validated that they will imagine encounters and call them real. It's almost as if they give themselves over to their own imagination and call it visions and dreams, etc.

3. **Demonic encounters**: Demonic persuasion or experiences involving agents from the kingdom of darkness having access to the mystical through ignorance.

Symbolic Titles for Satan and Demons

To better understand how the Devil or his associates may operate or reveal themselves, below is a list of the Devil's common descriptions and appearances.

The Serpent

> *But I fear, lest somehow, as the serpent deceived Eve by his craftiness, so your minds may be corrupted from the simplicity that is in Christ.*
>
> **—2 Corinthians 11:3**

And I will put enmity between you and the woman, and between your seed and her Seed; He shall bruise your head, and you shall bruise His heel.

—**Genesis 3:15**

Behold, I give you the authority to trample on serpents and scorpions, and over all the power of the enemy, and nothing shall by any means hurt you.

—**Luke 10:19**

So the great dragon was cast out, that serpent of old, called the Devil and Satan, who deceives the whole world; he was cast to the earth, and his angels were cast out with him.

—**Revelation 12:9**

So the serpent spewed water out of his mouth like a flood after the woman, that he might cause her to be carried away by the flood.

—**Revelation 12:15**

And he cast him into the bottomless pit, and shut him up, and set a seal on him, so that he should deceive the nations no more till the thousand years were finished. But after these things he must be released for a little while.

—**Revelation 20:3**

THE GREAT RED DRAGON

So the great dragon was cast out, that serpent of old, called the Devil and Satan, who deceives the whole world; he was cast to the earth, and his angels were cast out with him.

—Revelation 12:9

He laid hold of the dragon, that serpent of old, who is the Devil and Satan, and bound him for a thousand years.

—Revelation 20:2

ANGEL OF LIGHT

And no wonder! For Satan himself transforms himself into an angel of light.

—2 Corinthians 11:14

ROARING LION

Be sober, be vigilant; because your adversary the devil walks about like a roaring lion, seeking whom he may devour.

—1 Peter 5:8

You shall tread upon the lion and the cobra, the young lion and the serpent you shall trample underfoot.

—Psalm 91:13

FOWLS OR BIRDS

And as he sowed, some seed fell by the wayside; and the birds came and devoured them.

—Matthew 13:4

When anyone hears the word of the kingdom, and does not understand it, then the wicked one comes and snatches away what was sown in his heart. This is he who received seed by the wayside.

—Matthew 13:19

SCORPIONS

Behold, I give you the authority to trample on serpents and scorpions, and over all the power of the enemy, and nothing shall by any means hurt you.

—Luke 10:19

WOLF

But a hireling, he who is not the shepherd, one who does not own the sheep, sees the wolf coming and leaves the sheep and flees; and the wolf catches the sheep and scatters them.

—John 10:12

FOWLER

Surely He shall deliver you from the snare of the fowler and from the perilous pestilence.

—Psalm 91:3

ADDER

You shall tread upon the lion and the cobra, the young lion and the serpent you shall trample underfoot.

—Psalm 91:13

CHAPTER SIX QUESTIONS

1. What is the difference between infatuation with the supernatural and desiring spiritual gifts?

_____

_____

_____

_____

_____

_____

2. Why is self-deception so dangerous and how can you avoid falling into this deception?

_____

_____

_____

_____

_____

_____

3. What is the angel of light looking for?

_____

_____

_____

_____

_____

_____

4. How do people give permission to "angels of deception" and give access to their lives?

_____

_____

_____

_____

_____

_____

Chapter Seven

CHRISTIAN MYSTICS

Metaphors reign where mysteries reside.

Unknown

Those who are carried off by fairy tales often wish to be. Let me explain. Those who desire spiritual experiences, above everything else, are destined for problematic encounters. Much like drug addicts, they need something to give them a fix.

When seeking encounters and experiences, there appears to be what I consider an "x-files" type of fascination with the unseen. This fascination, without the Word of God mixed with faith, is a groundwork for error.

This includes scenarios that are legitimate, at least to individuals who claim to have encountered them, such as the UFO narratives, obsession with a variety of conspiracies, and those who have seen these types of things. This is not to discount some of the things people say or even some conspiracies, as they are sometimes true! However, my grandfather would often say, "The main thing is that we keep the main thing, the main thing." This is the issue with many Christians who so desperately desire to escape the confines of this natural experience that they come to a place where truth is secondary to experiences. If something is mysterious and they have encountered it, new phrases and titles for a thing seem to arrive on the scene. Thus the saying, "Metaphors reign where mysteries reside." It is my hope to simply cause a love for the Word of God in this chapter, as there are many things taking place around the world with a variety of unique manifestations, and we should be looking at them only from the perspective of the Word of God and keeping our focus on the Lordship of Jesus Christ.

DO NOT ALLOW CONSPIRACIES TO HIJACK YOUR FAITH

Do not say, "A conspiracy," concerning all that this people call a conspiracy, nor be afraid of their threats, nor be troubled.

—Isaiah 8:12

Above is a great scripture to consider when dealing with conspiracies and unique issues. Notice it says, "Do not say 'A conspiracy' concerning all that this people call a conspiracy." In other words, do not run along with everything that is labeled a conspiracy—keep your head on straight! The follow-up exhortation in that same verse is also helpful: "Nor be afraid of their threats, nor be troubled."

Now, this doesn't mean that some conspiracies might not be true. As a matter of fact, it would seem that in our current world there are issues that only a few years ago were considered conspiracies but are now known information.

When people told us that our cellphones were listening to us and tracking our whereabouts, that was a conspiracy only a few short years ago; however, today it is normal and true. Things are so far down the road and advanced that we don't have just cellphones doing this! Now we have music devices in our homes that companies fully admit are recording us. This is simply an example, but it does show that not all conspiracies are false.

We must return to the firm foundation of the Word of God, no matter what comes our way. This generation will be exposed to more strange and weird phenomena than any generation before it. Christians who are prone to conspiracies and prone to the sensational, without having the reins of the Word of God governing their hearts, will fall prey to much of what is coming.

The Oxford Dictionary of the Christian Church explains the topic of mysticism by referencing mystical theology. This is interesting, as it sheds light on what many believers in Jesus Christ venture into.

> "Mysticism" generally refers to claims of immediate knowledge of Ultimate Reality (whether or not this is called "God") by direct personal experience; "mystical theology" is used to mean the study of mystical phenomena or the science of the mystical life. It has sometimes been suggested that such experience is the goal of all religion, and that there are certain experiences or patterns of experience which are common to believers in different religions or even in none, but this suggestion has been challenged on both philosophical and theological grounds. Paranormal phenomena, such as trances, visions and locutions, are often regarded as "mystical," though their value and significance is assessed differently by different thinkers; they are usually not regarded as essential.[2]

Christian mystics are those who will most likely fall for every wind of doctrine or new theory out there. The troubling issue regarding new theories and experiences is that without the Word of God many will be swept away into progressive deception.

Alien Encounter

Here is an example from our lives. One evening while my wife and I were staying high up in the mountains, Heather was woken up to a strange and somewhat horrific experience. She woke up to a voice speaking to her; she described it as if it was projected into her mind. The voice was saying, "Come out here." It was at this moment that our English mastiff began whining and crying outside the bedroom door. Heather got up and walked out of the bedroom, with this voice still speaking, and noticed our dog was hiding on the stairway facing the sliding doors to the front deck. She walked out to check on the dog and looked outside on the deck.

Now, it was about 3:00 AM and the only light that was on was our deck light because it was pretty remote in the wilderness. When she looked outside on the deck, something was standing there. It was the source of this projecting voice that had been saying, "Come out here." She described what she saw as a small humanoid creature with big, black eyes and gray skin, with the texture of a seal. It stood looking at her with its arms somewhat out from its sides, remaining very still and staring at her as it kept projecting the words, "Come out here." Heather was faced with a tremendous amount of fear; our dog, which was known to fight off bears and coyotes, was completely terrified while looking at this creature. Heather, who doesn't have much tolerance for fear, rose up in faith, with a hatred for the evil she was experiencing, and sat down next to our mastiff and began praying in the Holy Spirit. The next thing that happened as she glared back at it in faith was—it was gone.

I share this story only for the purpose of saying that we believe there are all kinds of wild things happening in our world at this time. However, we are not subject to any of them. Rather, we know that "greater is He that is in us than he that is in the world" (see 1 John 4:4). That little gray fella came knocking on the wrong door! How many other people might have played along with an entity like that?

In the last days, it is my personal opinion that things will begin to manifest more and more leading to an ultimate deception. The UFO alien phenomena will be a major player in that. The following scriptures from the book of Revelation may very well be speaking of alien-type creatures that will come upon the earth to deceive.

> *And I saw three **unclean spirits like frogs** coming out of the mouth of the dragon, out of the mouth of the beast, and out of the mouth of the false prophet. For they are **spirits of demons, performing signs, which go out to the kings of the earth and of the whole world**, to gather them to the battle of that great day of God Almighty.*
> —**Revelation 16:13-14**

The following scriptures could be applied to several things, including the false alien phenomena.

> *And there will be signs in the sun, in the moon, and in the stars; and on the earth distress of nations, with perplexity, the sea and the waves roaring; **men's hearts failing them***

from fear and the expectation of those things which are
coming on the earth, for the powers of the heavens will
be shaken.

—Luke 21:25-26

Notice how it says that men's hearts will fail them from fear and expectation of things which are coming on the earth. Then it reads further, saying, "The powers of the heavens will be shaken." The Bible doesn't specify what exactly it is that is coming upon the earth, but whatever it is will be observable and expected. Fear, to the point of heart attack, will be the result of such events. One could be a falsified alien invasion or visitation.

All paranormal encounters and the hysteria around them have a spirit of deception attached to them. This does not mean that what is coming will not be real; it simply means we must deal with it according to Isaiah 8:12, which says, "Nor be afraid of their threats, nor be troubled."

Application of the Word and prayer should be made to build your faith, not build conspiracies. For as the world gets stranger and stranger, many things will manifest. The alien scenario is simply one example.

THE HUMANISTIC LIE

Every *out-of-order experience* and *supernatural falsehood* is a result of a humanistic lie. Humanism is a point of view that places man over the things of God. A deception that says, "We don't need You, God." Humanism is also evil when it comes to deciphering spiritual encounters through the lens of your humanity rather than the Word of God.

When venturing into the supernatural, there is a protocol! Running after the unseen, without proper access, can cause catastrophic things to unfold in your life and affect many around you. This is the cause of many haunted houses, family curses, and other demonic points of entry. The worst thing is when foolish people try to communicate with the unseen realm, and like *brute beasts* become conduits for these dark celestial beings, allowing them permission and access to society. There is only one prescribed way we are to access the realm of the spirit and that is through the blood of Jesus Christ and the power of the Holy Spirit.

A FALSE ANOINTING

> *But the anointing which you have received from Him abides in you, and you do not need that anyone teach you; but as the same anointing teaches you concerning all things, and is true, and is not a **lie**, and just as it has taught you, you will abide in Him.*
>
> —1 John 2:27

The Greek word for *lie* is *pseudos* and can also be interpreted as false or falsehood. What this means is that there is a true anointing and a false anointing. Again, it looks like the real thing, but it is not—it's pseudo or false. This is a "form of godliness" or a way of operation that would lead those hearing to believe what they are experiencing is from God. Mystical Christians fall prey to false anointing all the time. It appeals to the five senses; it is what James 3:15 refers to as wisdom that does not descend from above but is earthly, sensual, and demonic. Stepping into the realm of experience and being open to just about anything can be a dangerous place to be.

A false anointing can be the result of encountering the real. Let me explain. When something legitimate is observed and the corresponding result is produced, those who do not know the spirit and have not paid the price for the anointing may attempt to manufacture what they have observed. A good example is found in Acts 18 when Peter came into contact with Simon the sorcerer. Simon had witnessed the power of the Spirit being transferred by the laying on of hands. Not knowing what to do, Simon asked if he could purchase the power!

> *And when Simon saw that through the laying on of the apostles' hands the Holy Spirit was given, he offered them money, saying, "Give me this power also, that anyone on whom I lay hands may receive the Holy Spirit." But Peter said to him, "Your money perish with you, because **you thought that the gift of God could be purchased with money!** You have neither part nor portion in this matter, for your heart is not right in the sight of God. Repent therefore of this your wickedness, and pray God if perhaps the thought of your heart may be forgiven you."*
>
> —Acts 8:18-22

Simon is the perfect example of someone not understanding the anointing and trying to attain it through his own carnal way. It is an interesting concept to consider that the Devil doesn't have an anointing, so he uses money. Think about that for a moment! The Devil doesn't possess God's supernatural anointing, so he is forced to use this natural system to accomplish his goals. This whole idea of a false anointing is dangerous territory and of great concern, as it can create a *snowball effect*. Once a mode or method is advanced that is not of God, yet is called a work of God, it has the potential of turning into a practice that is not rooted in God. The higher issue is when this involves spiritual encounters or experiences.

"Those who dance are thought mad by those who cannot hear the music." —Unknown

---

The above quote is a poetic way of saying *real inspiration is something not understood by those who do not possess it.* Where error lies is with those who would step out under the guise that they have heard the music, while all along neither they nor those following can hear anything.

When we don't understand a *thing*, religion comes along and attempts to fill in the blanks. Jesus spoke of this regarding Pharisees and their issue with making the Word of God ineffective by their traditions! There are certain experiences, or patterns of experience, which are common to believers in different religions.

Whenever there is an emphasis on experiences and spiritual beings that supersedes the gospel, there is an issue. Now, please hear me—there is a place for desiring spiritual gifts and the things of the spirit, but *never* should it take the place of the gospel. Of great concern is a culture now more interested in these things than good, healthy doctrine. By and large, believers have been exposed to less and less Bible, resulting in no bearing and no understanding of right and wrong. Ultimately, the biblically malnourished arrive at a place of little to no discernment at all, and the result is deception.

The kingdom of darkness does not mind one bit if these believers are caught up in desiring the supernatural. Believers baptized in the washing of the water of His Word are what darkness fears, as it is the Word of God and the Word of God alone that brings a right-sizing to spiritual encounters. Some might say, "Why is this such a concern and such a big deal?" The Word of God shows us that it is human nature to exchange the truth of God for a lie! This means, if we take anything over the Word of God as truth to navigate life, the lie will take hold—especially in the areas of spiritual things.

The good news is, if you are reading this right now, you can rise to your God-given potential in faith and discernment! Be encouraged, read your Bible, pray in the Spirit, and things will become clear for you. Do not be led along by every new wind of doctrine, nor every new experiential thing that comes along. Test the spirits by the Word of God, listen to ongoing healthy teaching, and you will have success navigating the new mystical things that seem to arrive on the playing field with every generation.

CORRECTION IS GOOD FOR YOUR SOUL

Whoever loves instruction loves knowledge, but he who hates correction is stupid.

—**Proverbs 12:1**

If you have a heart that looks for correction, you are wise. Correction should be through the Word of God as you are reading, from a trusted source like your pastor, or by a reputable leader in the Body of Christ. Don't be corrected by just anyone. This is a healthy practice and should be done by all believers, especially in the area of spiritual encounters.

CHAPTER SEVEN QUESTIONS

1. What makes a conspiracy dangerous?

_____

_____

_____

_____

_____

2. Using the Word of God, how should we examine a conspiracy and any experience shared with us?

_____

_____

_____

_____

_____

3. What is a humanistic lie?

_____

_____

_____

_____

4. How would you define a false anointing?

_____

_____

_____

_____

_____

5. Why is correction good for your soul?

_____

_____

_____

_____

_____

6. Has anyone ever brought a correction to you that was helpful?

_____

_____

_____

_____

_____

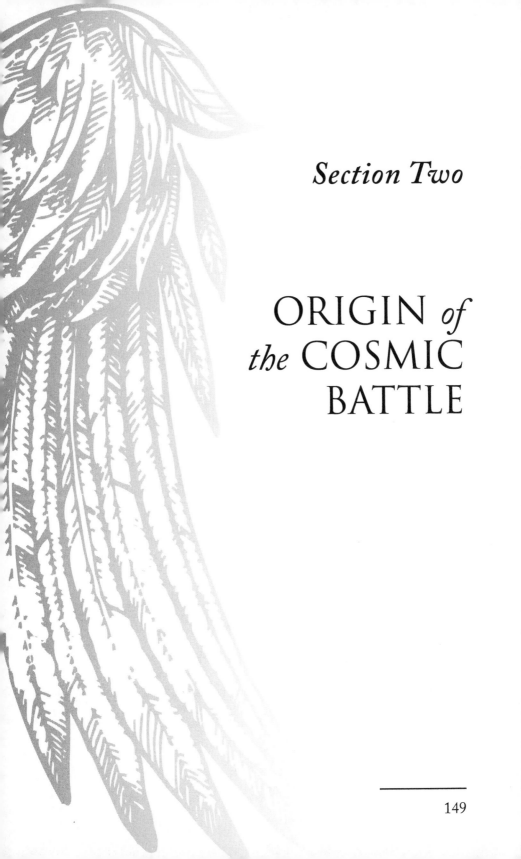

Section Two

ORIGIN *of* *the* COSMIC BATTLE

CELESTIAL HIERARCHIES *and* ANGELIC ORIGINS

For our God is a consuming fire.

Hebrews 12:29

od is a consuming *fire!* Angels are fiery servants. It is my
opinion that angels were created and drawn directly out of
the essence of God. Imagine it, these fiery flames pulled
directly out of the Consuming Fire Himself—forged by His Word
and operating as *autonomous extensions* of Himself!

Additionally, these are called *winds.* Wind represents the breath
of God. These *winds* are also an *extension of His breath!* Winds are
closely associated with His breath or voice.

The voice of the Lord divideth the flames of fire.
—Psalm 29:7 KJV

When the Lord speaks, He is speaking according to Psalm 29
and dividing these winds and flames of fire. *Dividing* carries the
connotation of commanding or releasing them on assignment.
Angels were created right from the very presence of God and are
part of His *fiery DNA.* They have their own thoughts and will;
however, being birthed straight from the fire of God, they are

to do what they are *built for.* Angels might also be referred to as highly intelligent spiritual beings not destined to be united with a human body. Differing from God's creation of man, these spiritual beings do not have a human soul but live out an immortal lifespan due to not possessing a physical body. Angels are spirits, and these were created to be God's companions in the kingdom of Heaven. Therefore, it was a terrible travesty when many of these created ones, in the beginning, *participated in Lucifer's mutiny!* How that must have hurt the heart of God as these creations of His were violating their very purpose and acted in complete betrayal of what they were built for.

CAN ANGELS STILL REBEL?

Angelic beings are fascinating, and we don't have a complete grasp on them as the Word of God only gives us glimpses of their behavior and operations. One example would be in the form of a question. How is it that angels once fell from grace, so to speak? And what assurances are there that the current forces of Heaven would not do what their former companions did when they rebelled against God? Well, the Word of God doesn't give us exact clarity on this issue; yet, we do get glimpses into how angels might respond as a whole to the temptation of receiving glory for themselves.

John the revelator, when exposed to an angelic messenger, fell down and began to worship the angel in Revelation 19. In a dramatic response, the angel said with urgency, "See that you do not do that! Worship God!" A glimpse of insight is revealed here. Let me explain. The Bible refers to an innumerable number of angels who still serve God; there was a smaller group of them who were deceived into rebelling against Him. Of the many who remained, they had the opportunity to witness the judgment pronounced on the rogue angels; it stands to reason that they had extreme clarity of the consequences for unrighteous acts of disobedience—gloomy dungeons, some buried, some placed into outer darkness. Even the angels imprisoned right now under the river Euphrates for the *day of judgment*, mentioned in the Book of Revelation, must have garnered the attention of the loyal hosts of Heaven. Any doubt was surely canceled out when they witnessed the creation of Hell and knew the location of the second death, known as *the lake of fire.*

These angelic warriors and messengers also witnessed the Church of Jesus, which is able to bind and loose spiritual forces in both Heaven and on Earth. Not to mention the casting out of demons and so much more. I am personally of the opinion that those who witnessed the rebellion and stood with integrity by the Lord God Almighty are thankful to the point of fear knowing what they would have been sentenced to had they followed the same path as their wicked brothers. If there is any thought of rebellion among angels today, it is certainly met with the reality of the punishment and fate they are privy to regarding fallen angels who left their proper abode. We will investigate more of this throughout the pages ahead.

Angelic ranking and order is something the Scripture reveals. What it likely offers is an insight into the way God's kingdom operates, much like a government with a military and police force. It could be that the purpose of many angelic and celestial beings was to oversee creation from the spiritual side of reality. This is recognizable even in the life of Lucifer before he gained the moniker *Satan*. He was the anointed cherub who covered. Ezekiel 28:14 (KJV), "Thou art the *anointed cherub* that covereth; and I have set thee so: thou wast upon the holy mountain of God; thou hast walked up and down in the midst of the stones of fire."

CELESTIAL HIERARCHIES

Authority and position were a part of the differing celestial beings. Today these positions in God's kingdom remain. What each position does and how they operate are only shown in small snapshots throughout Scripture. What we do know is that the Lord has set up His kingdom structure with various authorities and celestial responsibilities.

> *Far above all principality and power and might and dominion, and every name that is named, not only in this age but also in that which is to come.*
>
> **—Ephesians 1:21**

> *For by Him all things were created that are in heaven and that are on earth, visible and invisible, whether thrones or dominions or principalities or powers. All things were created through Him and for Him.*
>
> **—Colossians 1:16**

By referencing these two passages of Scripture, it shows *five different ranks were arrived at.* Their number and order were fixed by Dionysius (a theologian from the year AD 500). He laid out what he called *celestial hierarchies,* in which angelic entities were arranged into three hierarchies containing three choirs each, in the order of *seraphim, cherubim, and thrones; dominations, virtues, and powers; principalities, archangels, and angels.* He concluded that of these only the last two choirs have an immediate mission to men. In the Middle Ages, Dionysius' *speculative doctrine* was taken over and developed by others; a treatise on angels became a part of the commentaries on the *Sentences* of Peter Lombard from the 13th century onward.

Thomas Aquinas (theologian 1225–1274) taught an interesting point of view regarding the angelic will, meaning their choices and decisions. Aquinas, after much study and consideration, concluded that one good or bad act by an angelic entity *fixes him irrevocably* in good or evil. This must have been in reference to the original decision they were presented with to do good or evil. Additionally, most historical scholastics taught that the angels were created at the same time as the material universe and that they were *elevated to a state of grace* in order to undergo a *test* followed either by supernatural beatitude or eternal damnation; furthermore, that the divine mysteries, even the incarnation, were then revealed to them.[3]

Fascinating would be one way to describe the possibility of Aquinas' conclusions regarding angelic choices, as well as Dionysius' *celestial positions!* It is definitely an interesting consideration to ponder whether angels deciding to do good or bad is an original decision that set the course of their eternal destiny. It could be as these early theologians concluded, as well as what we have looked at in previous chapters—righteous angels, after witnessing what happened to their mutinous brothers, knew they had chosen wisely. As a result of this, they likely became fully persuaded by the light of God.

As to what the rank and file might be in the unseen realm, we can only go as far as the Word of God does. To fully embrace

Dionysius' *celestial positions* view would require a *level of speculation*, but it is still worth looking at. One thing we can stand on firmly is references to angelic figures Scripture does speak of. Below is a list of the ones clearly spoken of in Scripture.

SERAPHIM

> *Above it stood* **seraphim***; each one had six wings: with two he covered his face, with two he covered his feet, and with two he flew. And one cried to another and said: "Holy, holy, holy is the Lord of hosts; The whole earth is full of His glory!" And the posts of the door were shaken by the voice of him who cried out, and the house was filled with smoke. So I said: "Woe is me, for I am undone! Because I am a man of unclean lips, And I dwell in the midst of a people of unclean lips; For my eyes have seen the King, The Lord of hosts." Then one of the* **seraphim** *flew to me, having in his hand a live coal which he had taken with the tongs from the altar. And he touched my mouth with it, and said: "Behold, this has touched your lips; Your iniquity is taken away, and your sin purged."*
>
> —Isaiah 6:2-7

CHERUBIM

> *After he drove the man out, he placed on the east side of the Garden of Eden* **cherubim** *and a flaming sword flashing back and forth to guard the way to the tree of life.*
>
> —Genesis 3:24 NIV

THRONES

*Whether **thrones** or dominions or principalities or powers.*
—Colossians 1:16

DOMINION

*Far above all principality and power and might and **dominion**.*
—Ephesians 1:21

POWERS

*Whether thrones or dominions or principalities or **powers**.*
—Colossians 1:16

PRINCIPALITIES

*Far above all **principality** and power and might and dominion.*
—Ephesians 1:21

*Whether thrones or dominions or **principalities** or powers.*
—Colossians 1:16

ARCHANGELS

For the Lord Himself will descend from heaven with a shout, with the voice of an **archangel***, and with the trumpet of God. And the dead in Christ will rise first.*

—1 Thessalonians 4:16

Yet Michael the **archangel***, in contending with the devil, when he disputed about the body of Moses, dared not bring against him a reviling accusation, but said, "The Lord rebuke you!"*

—Jude 1:9

ANGELS

And of the **angels** *He says: "Who makes His angels spirits and His ministers a flame of fire."*

—Hebrews 1:7

But to which of the **angels** *has He ever said: "Sit at My right hand, till I make Your enemies Your footstool"? Are they not all ministering spirits sent forth to minister for those who will inherit salvation?*

—Hebrews 1:13-14

ENTITIES OF HIGHER SUBSTANCE

All created things—including spirit beings such as angels, cherubim, seraphim, and each above referenced—are a form of *spiritual material substance*. Some of these *substances* may potentially be of a higher form than others. Though it would seem that all are visible in their own realms or dimensions—when applying our understanding, the human experience of only seeing and perceiving our three-dimensional space—some of these dimensional spaces may not be visible to others of lower realms.

Spirit beings, for example, are of a higher substance than flesh and the ordinary, *corporeal* material that we can see. They are not limited to natural substances as we know them. Higher substance beings can go through closed doors, walls, and any material object. This is seen throughout Scripture and even in testimonies.

I'm grateful for the observations of the late Chuck Missler on the topic of dimensions. Here is a reference to the ten known dimensions.

> Space is not simply an empty vacuum. Isaiah 64:1 says it can be torn; Psalm 102 says it can be worn out like a garment; Hebrews 12:26, Haggai 2:6, and Isaiah 13:13 say it can be shaken; in 2 Peter 3:12, it can be "burnt up"; in Revelation 6:14, "it split apart like a scroll." Hebrews 1:12 says it can be "rolled up like a mantle." What is meant by "rolled up"? Let's think that through: in order for space to be rolled up, there must be some dimension in which it's thin. (If it's not thin, you can't roll it up.) Also, if it can be rolled up, it can

be bent. If it can be bent, there must be some *direction* toward which it can be bent. The whole idea of being rolled up implies thinness and an *additional dimension* in which to roll it up, which begins to indicate that space has more than three dimensions, which we now know today from particle physics.

But the Scripture has said all along that we have additional, spacial dimensions. Nachmonides, a Hebrew sage of the twelfth century, concluded from studying Genesis, chapter 1, that the universe has ten dimensions. Four of those are directly "knowable" and six of them are "not knowable" (in his vocabulary). Particle physicists in the 21st century now believe that the universe has ten dimensions but only four of them are directly measurable.[4]

The possibility of these ten dimensions, and the potential spiritual activity which may vary within them, is a very interesting thing to consider. After all, according to the above reference by Missler, regarding 21st-century particle physicists—the universe indeed has ten dimensions that we know about. Could it be that certain spiritual beings could be limited to their own dimension and only able to see *beneath them,* so to speak? What makes this concept interesting is that, according to Scripture, we know that the prince of this world was cast out. When Jesus was about to go to the cross, He made the statement in John 12:31, "Now is the judgment of this world; now the ruler of this world will be cast out." From where was the ruler of this world being cast out? The courts of Heaven. You see the Devil coming before the Lord with the angels to present themselves before Him. Satan had this access because it had been given to him by Adam and Eve when he deceived them. Of course, this was one of the main reasons Jesus came! To destroy the works of the Devil!

> *For this purpose the Son of God was manifested, that He might destroy the works of the devil.*
>
> —1 John 3:8

Where this logically takes us is to the question: Does this apply to the realm of darkness and the fallen angels? Yes, Ephesians 6 references this and was written after Jesus knocked the Devil out of his access to Heaven.

> *For we do not wrestle against flesh and blood, but against principalities, against powers, against the rulers of the darkness of this age, against spiritual hosts of wickedness in the heavenly places.*
>
> —Ephesians 6:12

> *In which you once walked according to the course of this world, according to the prince of the power of the air, the spirit who now works in the sons of disobedience.*
>
> —Ephesians 2:2

Although the Devil doesn't have full access to Heaven as he once did, he and the fallen angels, along with the demonic hordes, have a certain position on Earth. These seats of authority will not be fully removed until the Lord returns and binds the Devil for a thousand years and ultimately sentences him to the lake of fire.

What does this mean for the ranks of darkness today? Likely, they are a fallen mirror of angelic servants of light, only much less powerful and far weaker as they are no longer in alignment with the Lord of Heaven. As we listed several types and ranks of angelic, celestial beings in the kingdom of God, it very well could be that their counterparts function with the same mode of operation in the kingdom of darkness.

The best form of deliverance long term is great Bible teaching.

As stated, they don't have power by the name of Jesus; they also don't have the authority that believers, covered under the Blood of Jesus, possess. What they do have is territories, hearts, and minds under their persuasion, and that has proved to be quite effective throughout history.

When we recognize that we wrestle not against flesh and blood but against principalities, powers, and rulers of wickedness in high places, what we are really dealing with is their evil influence on free moral agents and giving these principalities and powers the ability to make decisions and run nations through their "hosts." Preaching the gospel is the highest and most potent form of breaking these strongholds. After that comes the renewing of the mind! The best form of deliverance long term is great Bible teaching.

When approaching the idea that there might be angelic beings in different classes or positioned apart from one another throughout these ten dimensions, this leads to interesting speculation. One thing we do know is that the vast majority of humans will not see beyond their natural five senses until they cross into eternity upon death. Most of mankind will remain limited to this three-dimensional experience, never encountering the other seven dimensions beyond them.

> *For I am persuaded that neither death nor life, nor angels nor **principalities** nor **powers**, nor things present nor things to come, nor height nor depth, nor **any other created thing**, shall be able to separate us from the love of God which is in Christ Jesus our Lord.*
>
> —Romans 8:38-39

So, what is the conclusion about ranks and levels of angelic, celestial authority? The answer remains the same. Preach the gospel, win as many as you can, and make disciples by the Word of God! Understand also, when engaging in prayer and walking out what God has assigned you to do in this life, it is the great love of God that you cannot be separated from!

SERVANTS *of* FIRE

CHAPTER EIGHT QUESTIONS

1. What do you think is keeping angels from rebelling against
   God again?

   _____

   _____

   _____

   _____

   _____

2. How many dimensions have been discovered?

   _____

   _____

   _____

   _____

   _____

3. List the different types of angelic figures.

   _____

   _____

   _____

   _____

   _____

164

4. What is the conclusion about ranks and levels of angelic, celestial authority?

_____

_____

_____

_____

_____

_____

Chapter Nine

BECOMING *the* PRINCE *of* DARKNESS

In the beginning…

Genesis 1:1

When considering the creation of the universe, there is much to be *deciphered*. I'm going to present a possible narrative in a story form that potentially explains why the Devil came into existence—from Lucifer to Satan. It is short and colorful, but I believe it will drive the point home.

A BRIEF STORY OF CREATION

At the very beginning, before time was measurable, before stars, before mountains and seas, and well before man was on the planet, I imagine an epoch in which the Creator of all things was looking far into the distance, His thoughts were fixed, and the sense of destiny was palpable. I like to imagine one of the angelic hosts standing near Him asking, "Lord, what are You gazing at in such a captivated manner?" "You will see," replied the great God of the universe.

At this statement, the sons of God knew something was happening and began gathering together. Something was certainly stirring. There was excitement in the air; something was happening that they had never witnessed in all of their existence. The *Ancient of Days* stepped forward with His attention directed at the void stretched out before them all. He paused, then spoke, "Stars be!" and stepping forward, He swung His arm in a sweeping motion from left to right, while simultaneously opening His powerful hand and flinging a variety of burning lights far out into the void. Each light found its place and began to brighten and shine from deep within the void.

When the sons of God saw the radiant lights throughout the void, they shouted with joy! They had never seen anything like this. He looked at them, smiled, and said, "Do you like it?" "Yes!" they cried. He then said, "It's all still moving out there—it will continue expanding forever." With this knowledge, all of the angels' eyes became intent with expectation.

Now turning His attention to a closer area of this starry void, He began to create. His demeanor and approach were much like that of an artist painting on a canvas. His focus and gaze were fixed on a particular area as He began to place planets, moons, meteors, and one particular star in a localized space. He called the single star the *sun* and the other prominent light He named the *moon*. Upon this nomenclature, His audience of angels went wild! He then turned to them all, saying, "Watch!" Suddenly, as if zooming in on a map, they all together went from the void of space to hovering above a planet covered in water. The Lord began calling dry land to "Appear" and aquatic life to "Be." Land creatures of all sizes—birds, giraffes, and herds of wild stallions—were suddenly running across the open plains. Shouting and praises once again erupted among the sons of God! They began jumping up and down, releasing exuberant shouts of joy and praising God. A moment like this had never happened before and these sons of God were absolutely overwhelmed by what they were witnessing.

*When the morning stars sang together, and **all the sons of God shouted for joy?***

—Job 38:7

About this time, one of the prominent angels was flying by. This entire event had captured his attention; he was intrigued by all the activity. He landed near the Lord along with the angels who were now standing on the earth. It was at this moment that the Lord of Hosts, the God of Creation, the Great I AM, said, "I've saved the best for last...."

The Lord kneeled and placed His hands into the dirt. The prominent angel was suddenly captivated by this moment and asked, "What are You doing?" "You will see," replied the Lord, with great pleasure on His countenance. His mighty hands began to form an image from the dirt He had placed His hands into; He was forming a body—a man. Lucifer, the angel asking questions, said, "I don't like this!" The Lord paid no attention to Lucifer's statement and continued until, finally, He opened the mouth of this dirt figure, and as He did, the great God of the universe breathed in deeply with one magnificent breath—then He released His very essence into the newly molded soil. The soil suddenly inhaled, eyes opened, and the dirt began to stand to its feet—now alive.

Lucifer examined this new being called man. He quickly and impatiently studied everything about this dirt figure that was now standing and breathing. Suddenly, he stepped back with horror. His face filled with disgust as he looked at God, the Father, and said, "This thing reminds me of something. It walks and talks. It is made of lowly dirt, yet I am deeply reminded of something." The Lord said, "What is it?" Lucifer replied, "It reminds me of, I can't help but notice... no... it cannot be, how!?" Now visibly shaken Lucifer cried out, "This is not possible, it's only dirt! *It reminds me of You!*"

God said, "Why yes, this is My son. His name is Adam."

> *And God said, Let us make man in our image, after our likeness: and let them have dominion over the fish of the sea, and over the fowl of the air, and over the cattle, and over all the earth, and over every creeping thing that creepeth upon the earth. So God created man in his own image, in the image of God created he him; male and female created he them.*
>
> —Genesis 1:26-27 KJV

Lucifer had a realization at this moment, a realization of what had just transpired. He now recognized that God had just placed His very breath and image within the dirt. What this meant for Lucifer was that God had just placed dirt above him! Dirt was now exalted above Lucifer! As we have looked at earlier, Psalm 8:4-5 says that man was made a little lower than the angels. However, the actual Hebrew word the translators used was *Elohim*, a Hebrew word translated as "God" more than 2,600 times in the Old Testament that designates the one true God.

> *What is man that You are mindful of him, and the son of man that You visit him? For you have made him a little lower than the angels, and You have crowned him with glory and honor.*
>
> —Psalm 8:4-5

LUCIFER'S RAGE

At that moment, Lucifer, now trembling with rage, cried out! *"How dare You! How could You! I hate it! I will kill it!"* Because of this, war broke out as Lucifer began to explain to many angels that God had demoted them from their rightful place. Michael, the warring archangel, stood up, gathered angels faithful to God the Father, and collided with the rebellious horde of angels who went rogue.

Michael and his angels cast them out of their access to Heaven. Thus began the saga of light versus darkness, with mankind in the balance. The epic levels of violence, atrocities, and evil experienced throughout history stem from this moment. It is sad to realize that God did not create Adam to endure such things. He was created for fellowship, for family. When the Lord walked with Adam in the cool of the day, He built a relationship with Adam. It was never His plan to see evil come upon creation or on His son and daughter, Adam and Eve. The good news is God was not outmatched and cannot be outwitted. Jesus would come one day as the Last Adam and change everything.

LUCIFER'S CONTEMPT

Of judgment, because the ruler of this world is judged.
                                        —John 16:11

Lucifer's contempt was something he birthed in his own heart from the beginning of his existence. Jesus called the Devil "a murderer from the beginning," and "the father of liars" in John 8:44. In the Book of Revelation, John the apostle makes it abundantly clear that the dragon mentioned is "that serpent of old" also known as the Devil or Satan.

*So the great dragon was cast out, **that serpent of old**, called the Devil and Satan, who deceives the whole world; he was cast to the earth, and his angels were cast out with him.*
—Revelation 12:9

*He laid hold of the dragon, that **serpent of old**, who is the Devil and Satan, and bound him for a thousand years.*
—Revelation 20:2

The Devil led a conflict that erupted among the angelic ranks within Heaven's armies, and it was all over humanity. It is a fascinating thing to consider that these angelic beings believed Lucifer over God to the point that war erupted. This has often led me to ask the question, "Why would God allow this? How is it that these angels could think in this fashion?" Students of the Word of God can get glimpses of why the Devil was so angry.

Let's consider a passage from Job 1, in which we find Satan coming before God among the "sons of God." The terminology "sons of God" is the Hebrew word *b'nai Elohim* and carries the meaning that these angels are a direct creation of God. This is referencing the angels present before God's throne. The same reference is used again in Job 38:7 when *the sons of God shouted for joy at the creation of the world.*

Angels enjoyed the status of being direct creations of God the Father Himself. There was nothing like them until He created the first man. Adam was also a direct creation of God, but that is not all! Adam was made in God's image and likeness because he had the very breath of God within him! This set him apart from the angels who, although they were themselves direct creations of God, did not carry His image and likeness as Adam did. As a result, this may have been the main point the Devil used to accuse God to the angels who believed his lies. We will talk further about the ramifications of their rebellion in the pages ahead.

THE BEGINNING

In the beginning was the Word, and the Word was with God, and the Word was God.

—John 1:1

Before we explore deeper into angels, let's go back to the beginning for a moment. It must have been astonishing in the beginning! Just imagine it.

God in "eternity past" thinking about you. There was peace, there was stillness, there was fulfillment. God, the great I AM, most likely had never experienced sorrow or an angry thought up to this time. He considered the future within His inner image, marinating on what would come. Greater clarity is shown to us in John 1:1, where Scripture speaks of "eternity past" by using the terminology, "the Word was with God." This phrase "was with" is the Greek word *pros,* which means "toward," and in this case it means "toward one another" or "face to face." Another way of saying it would be that God the Father and the pre-incarnate Son looked into each other's countenance throughout "eternity past." What were They thinking about? I believe it is possible They were planning the existence of creation and the dramatic story arc of mankind.

Scripture reveals that Jesus was going to be crucified ever since the foundation of the world. As Revelation 13:8 says, Jesus was, "The Lamb slain from the foundation of the world." Think about that! God the Father and Jesus the Son knew not only what was within each other, but They knew that mankind would fall, that angels would *rebel*, and that the only way of redemption would be Jesus offering Himself. They knew this from the foundation of the world! More amazingly, They chose to create it all despite the issues that would surely come. Why? Because They wanted to know you.

> *Looking unto Jesus, the author and finisher of our faith, who for the joy that was set before Him endured the cross, despising the shame, and has sat down at the right hand of the throne of God.*
>
> **—Hebrews 12:2**

Additionally, the Son knew that from Him (God the Father) to Him and through Him are all things. Thus, the Son would only do what He saw His Father doing.

> *For of Him and through Him and to Him are all things, to whom be glory forever. Amen.*
>
> **—Romans 11:36**

JESUS—THE VOICE OF GOD

The Father is the source, the One who so loves the Son and through Him would love all that would come in "eternity future." It must have been a pleasant moment for Them when the time came to manifest what They had imagined together. The inner essence of the Father desired to create what was already a reality on the inside. There was only one way to release it—to speak. His voice was found in His Son. Through Him, that is Jesus, the worlds would be formed because He is the exact representation of God the Father—especially in word form.

Dear reader, never forget you were the joy set before Him as He went to the cross.

In my mind, I see it like this: "Let there be light!" was uttered, and the sound of that voice came through the Son, and light was. Jesus, the Word made flesh, Jesus was that same "Word with God" in the beginning. Jesus was the "Master Craftsman" beside God the Father, creating the world. The Father speaking through the Son, crafting the world. Jesus is the voice of God!

The Lord possessed me at the beginning of His way, before His works of old. I have been established from everlasting, from the beginning, before there was ever an earth. When there were no depths I was brought forth, when there were no fountains abounding with water. Before the mountains *were settled, before the hills, I was brought forth; while as yet He had not made the earth or the fields, or the primal dust of the world. When He prepared the heavens, I was there, when He drew a circle on the face of the deep, when He established the clouds above, when He strengthened the fountains of the deep, when He assigned to the sea its limit, so that the waters would not transgress His command, when He marked out the foundations of the earth, then **I was beside Him as a master craftsman**; and I was daily His delight, rejoicing always before Him, rejoicing in His inhabited world, and my delight was with the sons of men.*

—**Proverbs 8:22-31**

It is profound to realize that from the time of creation through the Son, to the moment of jealousy and rage that filled Lucifer, God the Father and Jesus the Son had a rescue mission in place for the redemption of man. From man's fall to redemption, God, knowing all things that would transpire, still chose to move forward with creation and the plan for "eternity future"! The angels saw it all; they observed every scenario between the divine Father and the fallen creation. On each side of the issue, both good and evil, these angelic entities are woven into the narrative having a part to play in this cosmic saga. Curiosity or contempt are issues depending on which angelic messengers are involved.

CHAPTER NINE QUESTIONS

1. Why do you think the Devil hated man so much?

_____

_____

_____

_____

_____

_____

2. Why do you think some angels followed Satan and rebelled against God?

_____

_____

_____

_____

_____

_____

3. What was God's rescue plan for humanity?

_____

_____

_____

_____

_____

_____

4. How was Jesus (the Word) part of creation?

_____

_____

_____

_____

_____

_____

Chapter Ten

ENOCH *and*
the FALLEN ANGELS

And Enoch walked with God after he begat Methuselah three
hundred years, and begat sons and daughters: and all the days
of Enoch were three hundred sixty and five years: and Enoch
walked with God: and he was not; for God took him.

Genesis 5:22-24 KJV

E noch is a fascinating character when you consider his story and
prophetic utterances quoted in the New Testament by Jude,
Jesus, and others. He was seventh from Adam and he had a
unique place in history as one who, "*Walked* faithfully with God;
then he was no more, because God took him away" (see Genesis
5:24 NIV). This narrative leaves a lot to the imagination. However,
even though there are many things debatable and even potentially
illegitimate within the Book of Enoch, there are certainly other
writings within its pages that should not simply be dismissed out
of hand.

> *By faith Enoch was translated that he should not see*
> *death; and was not found, because God had translated*
> *him: for before his translation he had this testimony, that*
> *he pleased God. But without faith it is impossible to please*

him: for he that cometh to God must believe that he is, and
that he is a rewarder of them that diligently seek him.

—Hebrews 11:5-6 KJV

And Enoch also, the seventh from Adam, prophesied of
these, saying, Behold, the Lord cometh with ten thousands
of his saints.

—Jude 1:14 KJV

There are references to events and scenarios in the Book of Enoch that, although it is not *canon* or part of Scripture, it does offer some interesting possibilities. We won't cover all of these; however, what we are going to look at may give deeper insight into a greater scope of the story arc of angelic beings. The good, the bad, and the future that is to come regarding these beings.

Considering the Book of Enoch

To build up to the narrative regarding angels, let's consider a few points of interest regarding the Book of Enoch. There are areas of controversy surrounding the book, yet several things are worth noting. Portions of it were discovered in the caves at Qumran not too long after the end of World War II. Upon this discovery, it was revealed that the Book of Enoch survives in its most complete form in *Ethiopic*, a Semitic language formerly spoken in Ethiopia, and is still used today as the liturgical language of the Christian church in Ethiopia. Much of the issue scholars have with the book is due to large portions of it that are most likely *pseudepigrapha*, or writings that were credited to someone other than the real author or potentially falsely written. The book embodies a series of revelations, of which Enoch is the recipient, on such matters as the origin of evil, angels, and the nature of Gehenna and Paradise. Regardless of the areas scholars feel are *pseudepigrapha*, the Book of Enoch should still carry value to those interested in biblical history, as it is directly quoted in the New Testament by Jude 1:14-15 and themes of Enoch are referenced in 2 Peter 2.

There are issues with the book and big questions about the actual author and the authenticity of some of its chapters, as you will see in a moment. Here are some valuable points that shed light on the authentic parts of the book. The first 36 chapters have long been considered Scripture in the Ethiopic Coptic Church (a church that claims the apostle John as its founder). Additionally, it was one of the most significant Jewish *pseudepigrapha* (writings ascribed to someone other than the real author). It was also known and commonly read in the Jewish culture when Jesus was a child.

There are those who argue that the Book of Enoch should be part of Scripture and included in the canon of the Bible. They cite a long-held belief by some that "the Book of Enoch was taken out of the Jewish canon by the Sanhedrin just after Jesus' death because of the prophecies they thought pointed to Jesus as the Messiah."[5] However, *The Oxford Dictionary of the Christian Church* states:

> This view has been increasingly questioned, especially since the discovery of the Qumran fragments [where the Dead Sea Scrolls were found]; for although all the other sections of 1 Enoch are well represented in these fragments, [the messianic] chapters 37–71 are not represented at all. Nor are they represented in the

Greek and Latin fragments. It is probable, therefore, that they are a later (Christian) insertion into the Book and that it was the New Testament which influenced them rather than vice versa.[6]

There is no question, however, that the chapters outside chapters 37–71 are before the time of Christ in their origin, as they were part of the fragments in Qumran. To make that point further, here are some direct Book of Enoch references quoted from the New Testament.[7]

Jesus referred to the Book of Enoch. Below are some scriptures, followed by the verse in Enoch they are pulled from:

Blessed are the meek, for they shall inherit the earth.

—Matthew 5:5

The elect shall possess light, joy and peace, and they shall inherit the earth.

—Enoch 5:7 {6:9}

But woe unto you that are rich! for ye have received your consolation.

—Luke 6:24 KJV

Woe to you who are rich, for in your riches have you trusted; but from your riches you shall be removed.

—Enoch 94:8 {93:7}

You who have followed Me will also sit on twelve thrones,
judging the twelve tribes of Israel.

—Matthew 19:28

I will place each of them on a throne of glory.

—Enoch 108:12 {105:26}

Between us and you there is a great gulf fixed.

—Luke 16:26

By a chasm…their souls are separated.

—Enoch 22: 9,11{22:10,12}

That ye may be the children of light.

—John 12:36 (KJV)

The good from the generation of light.

—Enoch 108:11 {105: 25}

Here is the most direct quote in the New Testament from the
Book of Enoch. It is by Jude, a brother of Jesus Christ:

And Enoch also, the seventh from Adam, prophesied of
these, saying, Behold, the Lord cometh with ten thousands
of his saints, to execute judgment upon all, and to convince
all that are ungodly among them of all their ungodly deeds

> *which they have ungodly committed, and of all their hard*
> *speeches which ungodly sinners have spoken against him.*
> —Jude 1:14-15 KJV, quoting Enoch 1:9

The point I am getting at is when the facts are accumulated, the Book of Enoch contains historical and even prophetic aspects to it, although it is not canon. Having made that statement, let me follow up with this. *We can never go beyond what is written in the actual canon of Scripture,* and I wholeheartedly believe the canon of the inspired Word of God is *closed*. Nothing can be added to it. However, on a historical, prophetic, and even speculative level, there are considerations and the possibility for answers not fully disclosed in the canon.

Over the next several pages I list segments directly from the Book of Enoch for the purpose of shedding some light on areas that may benefit you. Some points of view you may not have heard before will bring clarity or answers from the *realm of possibility*— such as the origin of angels, where demons came from, and several other helpful insights into how the angelic operates. As we look at these possibilities by reading the pages ahead directly from the Book of Enoch, please remember that *the Word of God is the final authority* and what we will look at will *never* carry more weight than God's Word.

The first few chapters of Enoch are fascinating, to say the least. These also fill in the blanks for the narrative in Genesis 6. In that chapter, we are introduced to a narrative that has been very difficult for many scholars from generations past. To summarize, we see angels who look down and see that the daughters of men were fair. At face value, it would seem that they came down and had relationships with them sexually. As a result, there were what the

Bible calls giants or men of renown—*the Nephilim*. These giants were indeed the offspring of angels that mixed their celestial flesh with the flesh of terrestrial women.

Goliath, whom David fought, along with Goliath's four brothers just as big as he was, was part of this same bloodline. It is my opinion that these giants spoken of in the Bible were the basis for Greek myths such as Hercules and the giant cyclops, Jack and the Beanstalk, as well as a variety of other monster stories. Part of the entire issue regarding Noah and the ark and God flooding the entire world was to destroy that polluted bloodline. This is also why Sodom and Gomorrah were to be destroyed.

These all were polluted by what the fallen angels and Satan had introduced to the earth. Why would they do such a thing? First, but of lesser importance is because they hated humanity, and second, but of greater importance is because of the prophecy spoken by God Himself to the serpent Satan in the garden, saying, "He will crush your head, and you will strike his heel" (see Gen 3:15 NIV). Satan knew, along with his rogue fallen angels, that this deliverer was to come through the children of humanity. These *nefarious rebels* decided to act on God's prophecy before it could come to pass. To accomplish this, they decided to poison the bloodline of humanity with their own seed! This way the Messiah and their doom would not be possible. They would remain in power over Earth and its inhabitants forever. Enoch recounts this in his book.

INSIGHT FROM THE BOOK OF ENOCH

The Book of Enoch tells the story of the watchers, or angels who watched over the earth. Rather than keep their position of watching over the earth, they began to watch the women at that time, lusting after them, and according to the Book of Enoch and Genesis 6, this resulted in these angelic watchers having sexual relations with them. There are those who have suggested there is a deeper meaning here. What might have actually taken place is tampering with the DNA of women, resulting in the birth of monstrous giants. *This is speculative but worth mentioning.*

Below are a few chapters directly taken from the Book of Enoch.[8] As you read the account, keep in mind that what these chapters hold was *mainstream* in the Jewish culture in Jesus' day. A few questions may be answered for you regarding why Jude speaks of angels who did not keep their proper position and are held in gloomy dungeons until the day of judgment. By not keeping their proper position, it is referencing the actions of the wicked angels who set out to poison the entire bloodline of humanity. *It is also interesting that neither Lucifer nor Satan is mentioned in the chapters presented here.* It could be that he was causing mischief elsewhere during the time of this narrative. Interestingly, the angels who stepped into this error were dealt with by imprisoning them in *gloomy dungeons.* Not even the Devil has been bound up in a gloomy dungeon. Nonetheless, the actions taken by these fallen *watchers* are a result of Satan sinning against God. While reading through the brief chapters of Enoch, there can be a sense of dread, especially when you do not have a close relationship with the living God. As you read this, look at it through a lens of possibility, not as if it were Scripture.

ENOCH 6

And it came to pass when the children of men had mul-
tiplied that in those days were born unto them beautiful

and comely daughters. And the angels, the children of the heaven, saw and lusted after them, and said to one another: "Come, let us choose us wives from among the children of men and beget us, children." And Semjâzâ, who was their leader, said unto them: "I fear ye will not indeed agree to do this deed, and I alone shall have to pay the penalty of a great sin." And they all answered him and said: "Let us all swear an oath, and all bind ourselves by mutual imprecations not to abandon this plan but to do this thing." Then sware they all together and bound themselves by mutual imprecations upon it. And they were in all two hundred; who descended [in the days] of Jared on the summit of Mount Hermon, and they called it Mount Hermon because they had sworn and bound themselves by mutual imprecations upon it. And these are the names of their leaders: Sêmîazâz, their leader, Arâkîba, Râmêêl, Kôkabîêl, Tâmîêl, Râmîêl, Dânêl, Êzêqêêl, Barâqîjâl, Asâêl, Armârôs, Batârêl, Anânêl, Zaqîêl, Samsâpêêl, Satarêl, Tûrêl, Jômjâêl, Sariêl. These are their chiefs of tens.

ENOCH 7

*And all the others together with them took unto themselves wives, and each chose for himself one, and they began to go in unto them and to defile themselves with them, and they taught them charms and enchantments, and the cutting of roots, and made them acquainted with plants. And **they became pregnant**, and **they bare great giants**, whose **height was three thousand ells**: Who consumed all the acquisitions of men. And when men could* *no longer sustain them,* **the giants turned against them and devoured mankind.** *And they began to sin against birds, and beasts, and reptiles, and fish, and to devour one another's flesh, and drink the blood.* *Then the earth laid accusation against the lawless ones.*

ENOCH 8

And Azâzêl taught men to make swords, and knives, and shields, and breastplates, and made known to them the metals (of the earth) and the art of working them, and bracelets, and ornaments, and the use of antimony, and the beautifying of the eyelids, and all kinds of costly stones, and all coloring tinctures. *And there arose much godlessness, and they committed fornication, and they were led astray, and became corrupt in all their ways.* **Semjâzâ taught enchantments, and root-cuttings, Armârôs the resolving of enchantments, Barâqîjâl, (taught) astrology, Kôkabêl the constellations, Ezêqêêl the knowledge of the clouds, (Araqiêl the signs of the earth, Shamsiêl the signs of the sun), and Sariêl the course of the moon.** *And as men perished, they cried, and their cry went up to heaven...*

ENOCH 9

And then Michael, Uriel, Raphael, and Gabriel looked down from heaven and saw much blood being shed upon the earth, and all lawlessness being wrought upon the earth. And they said one to another: "The earth made *without inhabitants cries the voice of their crying up to the gates of heaven. [And now to you, the holy ones of heaven], the souls of men make their suit, saying, 'Bring our cause before the Most High.'" And they said to the Lord of the ages: "Lord of lords, God of gods, King of kings, (and God of the ages), the throne of Thy glory (standeth) unto all the generations of the ages, and Thy name holy and glorious and blessed unto all the ages! Thou hast made all things, and power over all things hast Thou: and all things are naked and open in Thy sight, and Thou seest all things, and nothing can hide itself from Thee. Thou seest what Azâzêl hath done, who hath taught all unrighteousness on earth and revealed the eternal secrets which were (preserved) in heaven, which men were striving to learn: And Semjâzâ, to whom Thou hast given authority to bear rule over his associates. And they have gone to the daughters of men upon the earth, and have slept with the women, and have defiled themselves, **and revealed to them all kinds of sins.** And the women have borne giants, and the whole earth has thereby been filled with blood and unrighteousness. And now, behold, **the souls of those who have died are crying and making their suit to the gates of heaven,** and their lamentations have ascended: and cannot cease because of the lawless deeds which are wrought on the earth. And Thou knowest all things before they come to pass, and Thou seest these things and Thou dost suffer them, and Thou dost not say to us what we are to do to them in regard to these."*

ENOCH 10

Then said the Most High, the Holy and Great One spake,
and sent Uriel to the son of Lamech, and said to him:
"(Go to Noah) and tell him in my name 'Hide thyself!'
and reveal to him the end that is approaching: that the
whole earth will be destroyed, and a deluge is about to
come upon the whole earth, and will destroy all that is
on it. And now instruct him that he may escape and
his seed may be preserved for all the generations of
the world." *And again the Lord said to Raphael: "Bind*
Azâzêl hand and foot, and cast him into the darkness:
and make an opening in the desert, which is in Dûdâêl,
and cast him therein. And place upon him rough and
jagged rocks, and cover him with darkness, and let him
abide there forever, and cover his face that he may not
see light. And on the day of the great judgment he shall
be cast into the fire. And heal the earth which the angels
have corrupted, and proclaim the healing of the earth,
that they may heal the plague, and that all the children
of men may not perish through all the secret things that
the Watchers have disclosed and have taught their sons.
And the whole earth has been corrupted through the works
that were taught by Azâzêl: to him ascribe all sin." And
to Gabriel said the Lord: "Proceed against the bastards
and the reprobates, and against the children of fornica-
tion: and destroy [the children of fornication and] the
children of the Watchers from amongst men [and cause
them to go forth]: send them one against the other that
they may destroy each other in battle: for length of days

shall they not have. And no request that they (i.e. their fathers) make of thee shall be granted unto their fathers on their behalf; for they hope to live an eternal life, and that each one of them will live five hundred years." And the Lord said unto Michael: "Go, bind Semjâzâ and his associates who have united themselves with women so as to have defiled themselves with them in all their unclean-ness. And when their sons have slain one another, and they have seen the destruction of their beloved ones, bind them fast for seventy generations in the valleys of the earth, till the day of their judgment and of their consummation, till the judgment that is for ever and ever is consummated. In those days they shall be led off to the abyss of fire: (and) to the torment and the prison in which they shall be confined forever. And whosoever shall be condemned and destroyed will from thenceforth be bound together with them to the end of all generations. And destroy all the spirits of the reprobate and the children of the Watchers, because they have wronged mankind. Destroy all wrong from the face of the earth and let every evil work come to an end: and let the plant of righteousness and truth appear: [and it shall prove a blessing; the works of righteousness and truth] shall be planted in truth and joy for evermore. And then shall all the righteous escape, And shall live till they beget thousands of children, And all the days of their youth and their old age Shall they complete in peace. And then shall the whole earth be tilled in righteousness, and shall all be planted with trees and be full of blessing. And all desirable trees shall be planted on it, and they shall plant vines on it: and the vine which they plant thereon shall yield wine in abundance, and as for all the seed which is sown thereon each measure (of it) shall bear a thousand, and each measure of olives shall yield ten presses of oil. And cleanse thou the earth from all oppression, and from all unrighteousness, and from all sin, and from all godlessness: and all the uncleanness that is wrought upon the earth destroy from off the earth. [And all the children of men shall become righteous], and all nations shall offer adoration and shall praise Me, and all shall worship Me. And the earth shall be cleansed from all defilement, and from all sin, and from all punishment, and from all torment, and I will never again send (them) upon it from generation to generation and forever.

ENOCH 11

And in those days I will open the store chambers of blessing which are in the heaven, so as to send them down [upon the earth] over the work and labor of the children of men. And truth and peace shall be associated together throughout all the days of the world and throughout all the generations of men.

ENOCH 12

Before these things Enoch was hidden, and no one of the children of men knew where he was hidden, and where he abode, and what had become of him. And his activities had to do with the Watchers, and his days were with the holy ones. And I, Enoch was blessing the Lord of majesty

*and the King of the ages, and lo! the Watchers called me—
Enoch the scribe—and said to me: "Enoch, thou scribe of
righteousness, go, declare to the Watchers of the heaven
who have left the high heaven, the holy eternal place, and
have defiled themselves with women, and have done as
the children of earth do, and have taken unto themselves
wives: 'Ye have wrought great destruction on the earth:
And ye shall have no peace nor forgiveness of sin: and
inasmuch as they delight themselves in their children,* **The
murder of their beloved ones shall they see, and over the
destruction of their children shall they lament, and shall
make supplication unto eternity, but mercy and peace
shall ye not attain.'"**

ENOCH 13

*And Enoch went and said: "Azâzêl, thou shalt have no
peace: a severe sentence has gone forth against thee to put
thee in bonds: And thou shalt not have toleration nor
request granted to thee, because of the unrighteousness
which thou hast taught, and because of all the works of
godlessness and unrighteousness and sin which thou hast
shown to men." Then I went and spoke to them all together,
and they were all afraid, and fear and trembling seized
them. And they besought me to draw up a petition for
them that they might find forgiveness, and to read their
petition in the presence of the Lord of heaven. For from
thenceforward they could not speak (with Him) nor lift up
their eyes to heaven for shame of their sins for which they
had been condemned. Then I wrote out their petition, and*

the prayer in regard to their spirits and their deeds individually and in regard to their requests that they should have forgiveness and length (of days) And I went off and sat down at the waters of Dan, in the land of Dan, to the south of the west of Hermon: I read their petition till I fell asleep. And behold a dream came to me, and visions fell down upon me, and I saw visions of chastisement, [and a voice came bidding (me)] I to tell it to the sons of heaven, and reprimand them. And when I awaked, I came unto them, and they were all sitting gathered together, weeping in 'Abelsjâîl, which is between Lebanon and Sênêsêr, with their faces covered. And I recounted before them all the visions which I had seen in sleep, and I began to speak the words of righteousness, and to reprimand the heavenly Watchers.

ENOCH 14

*The book of the words of righteousness, and **of the reprimand of the eternal Watchers** in accordance with the command of the Holy Great One in that vision. I saw in my sleep what I will now say with a tongue of flesh and with the breath of my mouth: which the Great One has given to men to converse therewith and understand with the heart. As He has created and given [to man the power of understanding the word of wisdom, so hath He created me also and given] me the power of reprimanding the Watchers, the children of heaven. I wrote out your petition, and in my vision it appeared thus, that your petition will not be granted unto you [throughout all the days of* eternity, and that judgment has been finally passed upon you: yea (your petition) will not be granted unto you]. And from henceforth you shall not ascend into heaven unto all eternity, and [in bonds] of the earth the decree has gone forth to bind you for all the days of the world. And (that) previously you shall have seen the destruction of your beloved sons and ye shall have no pleasure in them, but they shall fall before you by the sword. And your petition on their behalf shall not be granted, nor yet on your own: even though you weep and pray and speak all the words contained in the writing which I have written. And the vision was shown to me thus: Behold, in the vision clouds invited me and a mist summoned me, and the course of the stars and the lightnings sped and hastened me, and the winds in the vision caused me to fly and lifted me upward, and bore me into heaven. And I went in till I drew nigh to a wall which is built of crystals and surrounded by tongues of fire: and it began to affright me. And I went into the tongues of fire and drew nigh to a large house which was built of crystals: and the walls of the house were like a tessellated floor (made) of crystals, and its groundwork was of crystal. Its ceiling was like the path of the stars and the lightnings, and between them were fiery cherubim, and their heaven was (clear as) water. A flaming fire surrounded the walls, and its portals blazed with fire. And I entered into that house, and it was hot as fire and cold as ice: there were no delights of life therein: fear covered me, and trembling got hold upon me. And as I quaked and trembled, I fell upon my face. And I beheld a vision, And lo! there was a second house, greater than the former, and *the entire portal stood open before me, and it was built of flames of fire. And in every respect it so excelled in splendor and magnificence and extent that I cannot describe to you its splendor and its extent. And its floor was of fire, and above it were lightnings and the path of the stars, and its ceiling also was flaming fire. And I looked and saw [therein] a lofty throne: its appearance was as crystal, and the wheels thereof as the shining sun, and there was the vision of cherubim. And from underneath the throne came streams of flaming fire so that I could not look thereon. And the Great Glory sat thereon, and His raiment shone more brightly than the sun and was whiter than any snow. None of the angels could enter and could behold His face by reason of the magnificence and glory and no flesh could behold Him. The flaming fire was round about Him, and a great fire stood before Him, and none around could draw nigh Him: ten thousand times ten thousand (stood) before Him, yet He needed no counselor. And the most holy ones who were nigh to Him did not leave by night nor depart from Him. And until then I had been prostrate on my face, trembling: and the Lord called me with His own mouth, and said to me: "Come hither, Enoch, and hear my word." [And one of the holy ones came to me and waked me], and He made me rise up and approach the door: and I bowed my face downwards.*

Enoch 15

And He answered and said to me, and I heard His voice: "Fear not, Enoch, thou righteous man and scribe of righteousness: approach hither and hear my voice. **And go, say to [the Watchers of heaven], who have sent thee to intercede [for them: 'You should intercede'] for men, and not men for you:** *'Wherefore have ye left the high, holy, and eternal heaven, and lain with women, and defiled yourselves with the daughters of men and taken to yourselves wives, and done like the children of earth, and begotten giants (as your) sons? And though ye were holy, spiritual, living the eternal life, you have defiled yourselves with the blood of women, and have begotten (children) with the blood of flesh, and, as the children of men, have lusted after flesh and blood as those [also] do who die and perish. Therefore have I given them wives also that they might impregnate them, and beget children by them, that thus nothing might be wanting to them on earth. But you were [formerly] spiritual, living the eternal life, and immortal for all generations of the world. And therefore I have not appointed wives for you; for as for the spiritual ones of the heaven, in heaven is their dwelling.* **And now, the giants, who are produced from the spirits and flesh, shall be called evil spirits upon the earth, and on the earth shall be their dwelling. Evil spirits have proceeded from their bodies; because they are born from men, [and] from the holy Watchers is their beginning and primal origin; [they shall be evil spirits on earth, and] evil spirits shall they be called. [As for the spirits of heaven, in heaven shall be their dwelling, but as for the spirits of the earth which were born upon the earth, on the earth shall be their dwelling.] And the spirits of the giants afflict, oppress, destroy, attack, do battle, and** *work destruction on the earth, and cause trouble: they take no food, [but nevertheless hunger] and thirst, and cause offenses. And these spirits shall rise up against the children of men and against the women, because they have proceeded [from them]."*

ENOCH 16

"From the days of the slaughter and destruction and death [of the giants], from the souls of whose flesh the spirits, having gone forth, shall destroy without incurring judgment—thus shall they destroy until the day of the consummation, the great [judgment] in which the age shall be consummated, over the Watchers and the godless, yea, shall be wholly consummated." And now as to the Watchers who have sent thee to intercede for them, who had been [aforetime] in heaven, (say to them): "You have been in heaven, but [all] the mysteries had not yet been revealed to you, and you knew worthless ones, and these in the hardness of your hearts you have made known to the women, and through these mysteries women and men work much evil on earth." Say to them therefore: "You have no peace."

The Book of Enoch is filled with many insights, none more interesting than how the Lord dealt with those rebellious celestial beings who, although they had an assignment, stepped out against God's plan for them and sought to violate God's most precious creation—mankind.

CHAPTER TEN QUESTIONS

1. Where were the first 36 chapters in the Book of Enoch discovered?

_____

_____

_____

2. Why did the fallen angels and the Devil want to pollute the bloodline?

_____

_____

_____

_____

_____

3. What was the judgment for these fallen beings?

_____

_____

_____

_____

_____

_____

4. What stands out to you as you read the chapters from the Book of Enoch?

_____

_____

_____

_____

_____

_____

Chapter Eleven

PRISON PLANET

How you are fallen from heaven, O Lucifer, son of the morning! How you are cut down to the ground, you who weakened the nations!

Isaiah 14:12

It is a fascinating realization to consider the Devil and all the fallen ones. These angels who left their proper abode are in all likelihood bound to Earth. It has become a prison planet for them. No longer can these ones enter into the realms of Heaven or the courts of the Lord. What is left for them to contemplate is a fiery end. *Judgment awaits these ones*, and yet it is plausible to believe they live in self-deception, thinking they will defeat the righteous in the end and lay claim to this Earth. After all, it was Lucifer who cried out he wanted all the worship!

> *How you are fallen from heaven, O Lucifer, son of the morning! How you are cut down to the ground, you who weakened the nations! For you have said in your heart: "I will ascend into heaven, I will exalt my throne above the stars of God; I will also sit on the mount of the congregation on the farthest sides of the north; I will ascend above the heights of the clouds, I will be like the Most High."*
>
> —Isaiah 14:12-14

Regarding what I am about to say, go to the Word of God. Keep the main thing the main thing. Whenever we take steps into arenas of speculation, it is vital that we do not force an issue and do what biblical studies label *eisegesis*—basically, the idea that a person injects their own ideas, beliefs, and philosophies into the text of Scripture rather than extracting what the Scripture is saying. This doesn't mean we cannot or should not consider looking into the possibilities. This is exactly what we will do when looking into the following scripture. Ezekiel 28 gives reference to what many scholars would agree is a passage regarding the Devil. Let's read the reference below and consider the possibilities.

You were in Eden, the garden of God; every precious stone was your covering: the sardius, topaz, and diamond, beryl, onyx, and jasper, sapphire, turquoise, and emerald with gold. The workmanship of your timbrels and pipes was prepared for you on the day you were created. You were the anointed cherub who covers; I established you; you were on the holy mountain of God; you walked back and forth in the midst of fiery stones. You were perfect in your ways from the day you were created, till iniquity was found in you. By the abundance of your trading you became filled with violence within, and you sinned; therefore I cast you as a profane thing out of the mountain of God; and I destroyed you, O covering cherub, from the midst of the fiery stones. Your heart was lifted up because of your beauty; you corrupted your wisdom for the sake of your splendor; I cast you to the ground, I laid you before kings, that they might gaze at you. You defiled your sanctuaries by the multitude of your iniquities, by the iniquity of your trading; therefore I brought fire from your midst; it devoured you, and I turned you to ashes upon the earth in the sight of all who saw you. All who knew you among the peoples are astonished at you; you have become a horror, and shall be no more forever.

—Ezekiel 28:13-19

First of all, it reads "You were in Eden." This cannot be talking about anyone else but Lucifer. Only three individuals were present in Eden—Eve, Adam, and the serpent. Now, there is much conjecture about the serpent. I take the conventional view that the serpent is indeed Lucifer, now becoming Satan because Adam and Eve gave him their position and seat of authority.

Second, notice it says, "You walked back and forth in the midst of the *fiery stones*." This is possibly a reference to the planets in our solar system.

Third, Ezekiel tells us iniquity was found in Lucifer. How? By the abundance of his trading. Why would it say, "the abundance of his trading"? It could be that before the fall, he was handling commerce on Earth, and the moment mankind was created he realized his position as the cherub who covered or oversaw this planet (or all the planets, a.k.a. "the stones of fire") was suddenly diminished. Lucifer was being put out of a job. Jealousy and rage took over, which caused him to rebel and destroy all of God's new rulers of Earth from Eden.

Fourth, Lucifer was cast down, as the remainder of the reference above in Ezekiel 28 states. Jesus, of course, makes mention of this moment:

And He said to them, "I saw Satan fall like lightning from heaven. Behold, I give you the authority to trample on serpents and scorpions, and over all the power of the enemy, and nothing shall by any means hurt you."

—Luke 10:18-19

Jesus says, "I saw Satan fall like lightning," His powerful statement regarding the Devil being cast out, but then adds, "I give you authority to trample on serpents and scorpions and over all the power of the enemy, and nothing shall by any means hurt you."

In the same moment, Jesus tells the disciples He witnessed Satan's fall, and continues by putting that instance into the same category as the authority we have been given over snakes and scorpions and over all the power of the enemy. Again, He might be referencing when these fallen angels, their demon cohorts, and all power they collectively possessed likely fell to Earth with Satan. Demons themselves were likely added to the mix later on. A fierce battle over Earth may be due to the fact that all these evil and dark forces have no other place to have influence over except Earth! *It is like a close-quarters arena, and these wicked beings want the territory.*

PRISON RULES

Outside of God's kingdom, these evil entities play by prison rules, meaning anything they can do to enslave mankind is what they will do! The Devil and all his forces are limited to a set of rules. Their rules are territorial. Whatever is given over to them is done by influence on the mind and ultimately cooperation in the natural. When a free moral agent submits their life to the Devil in any area, they have given territory to the kingdom of darkness. Most often this is done unknowingly. Darkness will hit you with an all-out assault on your emotions and your experiences to get you to crack. By "crack" I mean to agree with any way of thinking that opposes the written Word of God. When you violate the written Word of God in your thinking or actions, you are now a territory the Devil can operate through. However, through Jesus, His blood, and repentance, you can defeat that destructive access and territory by simply surrendering to Jesus and His words. Darkness doesn't play fair by our standards, but it must operate in a legal way, spiritually speaking. You see, you outrank evil spirits and fallen angels. You have God's very breath in you, and additionally you have a physical body on this Earth. The only way you as an individual can lose to the powers of darkness is to give them permission into your life. This begins with your thought life. Of course, this is why we take every thought captive to the obedience of Jesus Christ!

> *For though we walk in the flesh, we do not war according to the flesh. For the weapons of our warfare are not carnal but mighty in God for pulling down strongholds, casting down arguments and every high thing that exalts itself against the knowledge of God, bringing every thought into captivity to the obedience of Christ, and being ready to punish all disobedience when your obedience is fulfilled.*
> **—2 Corinthians 10:3-6**

Mind battles is one of the main points the above scripture is referencing. Darkness pushes and pushes with thoughts and emotional manipulation until you cave in and agree with it, letting those thoughts take hold.

Beat the prison rules set forward by the Devil and renew your mind to the written Word of God. Two things will happen:

1. Access by darkness will be denied.

2. You will experience angelic cooperation by being a vessel for the Word of God to be released into the Earth!

CHAPTER ELEVEN QUESTIONS

1. Have you ever considered that planet Earth is most likely a prison planet for the Devil?

   _____

   _____

   _____

2. How can you beat the prison rules set forth by the Devil?

   _____

   _____

   _____

   _____

   _____

   _____

3. What two things will happen once you do this?

   _____

   _____

   _____

   _____

   _____

4. What are some of the Devil's devices and how does he try to use them?

_____

_____

_____

_____

_____

_____

Chapter Twelve

HELL IS NOT ENOUGH

Then He will also say to those on the left hand, "Depart from Me, you cursed, into the everlasting fire prepared for the devil and his angels."

Matthew 25:41

When it comes to the topic of Hell and eternal punishment, the natural reaction by a thinking person is to often ask, *why?* Why would a loving God create such a horrible place? It seems over the top or unjust to many people. Individuals who are in a place of unquenchable fire and burning in the most horrendous agony imaginable. Some are able to reconcile the thought of mean, vile people going to such a place, but not kind, ordinary people who lived decent lives. Any notion of an eternal Hell could present a challenging thing to reconcile with the thoughts of loved ones, friends, or good people who may be headed there.

The topic of Hell is difficult to grapple with, especially when the truth of the matter is not presented correctly. Most people, even believers in Jesus, do not have a grasp on why such a severe eternal place would ever exist in the first place. Religion enters the narrative with *unhelpful tales* or *traditions* regarding Hell. This only misconstrues information about why people go there, or why in some cases there are exceptions for certain ones missing eternal damnation based on their good deeds.

More often than not religion uses guilt and manipulation about Hell to induce *behavior modification,* having little to do with the reality of the matter altogether. When talking about Hell, what I have found to be the most constructive point is: Why was it formed in the first place? The answer might surprise you. When understanding eternal punishment, we must first realize that Hell was not created for humanity. *It was created for Lucifer* and his band of rebellious fallen angels. These rogue sons of God acted against God in the most heinous way imaginable. Their attempt to hijack what God loved most was an act of vengeance against Him for His choice to exalt man above their celestial station. Lucifer's mutiny was not only the highest treason ever committed, it caused an angelic chain reaction of further mutiny against God. For this reason, war broke out in Heaven between Lucifer and his rogue forces in a collision with Michael, the archangel, and the forces of Heaven. We will look into this topic more in the pages ahead, but first let us come back to consider who God is.

THE PERFECTION THAT IS GOD

God is light, pure light, and there is not a trace of darkness in Him. God is all good; there is no evil in Him. We as humans relegate sin as bad actions or behaviors with consequences. Although this is correct, it is certainly not a complete picture. To mankind, sin has rank and severity. One sin is not as bad as another. An example would be telling a little white lie is not as bad in the eyes of most people as murdering someone is. Certain sins may be more grotesque than others to our natural minds and system of thinking. We as humans typically judge things based on *how we feel* about what was done. A judgment that involves our worldview, our cultural norms, values, what is acceptable in society, and how our experiences shaped what we believe to be good and bad. We grade on a curve based on subjective points of reference. Not God, because He is Spirit, as it says in John 4:24.

SIN IS SPIRITUAL

God is holy, and this doesn't mean He is only good and kind, etc. He doesn't choose to be holy. Rather, *He is holiness personified*. God has no darkness in Him. God's holiness is spiritual perfection of the highest order. Compared to God, there is nothing higher in holiness and perfection. Nothing can compare to Him. God has no equal to make a standard of Himself against; all He has is His Word. This is the reason when He made a promise to Abraham, He could swear by nothing greater, so He swore by Himself!

An understanding of the heights of God's perfection and unparalleled holiness is the beginning point of grasping *why Hell exists and lasts forever*.

Hell was a reaction. As Newton's third law of motion says, "With every action, there is an equal and opposite reaction." This was the case regarding the spiritual violation of God's holiness! A reaction happened! However, there is nothing in all existence to rise up as an equal to God's magnificence. A violation of God's holiness, by the mutiny of Lucifer, was the highest *spiritual violation* that had ever taken place! Think about it—this is why there will be a *new Heaven and new Earth*. Every place that was impacted by Lucifer's treachery will be done away with and recreated.

*Then I saw a great white throne and Him who sat on it, from whose face **the earth and the heaven fled away**. And there was found no place for them.*

—Revelation 20:11

*Then He who sat on the throne said, "**Behold, I make all things new.**" And He said to me, "Write: for these words are true and faithful."*

—Revelation 21:5

*Nevertheless we, **according to His promise, look for new heavens and a new earth in which righteousness dwells.***

—2 Peter 3:13

When the question is asked, "Why would a loving God send anyone to Hell?" the immediate answer should be that God doesn't send anyone to Hell. A proper response would be, if you knew the circumstances, you would recognize God is a victim of a crime that He chose to pay for! Additionally, Hell is not enough. Furthermore, Hell was not created for humanity! It is an angelic punishment. Yet, no matter how intensely and how furiously Hell burns, it will never suffice.

THE PUNISHMENT CANNOT PAY FOR THE CRIME

The devil, who deceived them, was cast into the lake of fire and brimstone where the beast and the false prophet are.

And they will be tormented day and night forever and ever.

—Revelation 20:10

It is true that the punishment is not enough to pay for the crime—this is why Hell burns *forever.* There have been those who have made statements over the years that are contrary to what the Bible teaches, such as, "Hell will come to an end because of love," or eventually Hell will be stopped because of the love of God. However, it's not about what God desires or what His will is; it is about action, reaction, and spiritual law. Might we suppose that God could have wiped out Adam and Eve the moment they sinned, as a result of their listening to the serpent? If so, then God the Father would have lost His kids forever. Adam and Eve were God's kids, and they, along with creation itself, were (in a sense) taken hostage by Satan. How? When Adam and Eve chose the word of the serpent over the Word of God, they immediately gave up the rights and authority they possessed to the one they chose to obey.

These two were to reign with dominion over the Garden and Earth. Subduing all creation was one of the assignments they were designated to operate in. Everything they had been entrusted with was given over to the Devil. He now had the authority and access to walk with God in the cool of the day or present himself along with the sons of God. Satan took creation hostage through the original sin of Adam and Eve. Rather than see His children destroyed, God chose to launch a rescue mission to save His family. It took hundreds of years of prophecy and obedience to see the prophetic statement God said, "You will bruise His heel, but He will crush your head" (see Genesis 3:15). God decided to go after His family, even at the cost of being rejected by them. He chose to allow us to have a choice by sending Jesus.

Now again, there have been teachers and preachers who claim Hell will not last for all eternity. Even if they mean well, they simply do not understand what the Scripture teaches. One day as I was thinking about these unbiblical claims, the realization came to me they were right! Hell will not last forever. Sadly and tragically, one day Hell and all its inhabitants will come to an end, of sorts. This will happen the day Hell and *everything within it* is cast into the lake of fire. Now, saying Hell will not last forever does not mean eternal punishment and damnation comes to an end. Rather, the exact opposite is true, and as horrifying as it is, damnation will increase in intensity and a heightened level of punishment that goes well beyond our capacity to understand.

> *Then Death and Hades were cast into the lake of fire. This is the second death.*
>
> **—Revelation 20:14**

Dreadful and horrifying is the thought of this moment. Every time I read this Scripture, it makes me hurt for the Lord. The only thing He doesn't have is the lost. I don't know about you, but I want to honor the Lord by pursuing the lost and bringing them home to Him. Leading people to salvation is one of the greatest ways to glorify God!

THE LAKE OF FIRE WILL LAST FOREVER

*And the **smoke of their torment ascends forever and
ever; and they have no rest day or night.***
—**Revelation 14:11**

The lake of fire is referred to as the "second death." Much of the
reasoning behind this title is that it likely is far more impossible
to describe than Hell itself. Hell is a place we can locate scriptural
descriptions of—not as much regarding the lake of fire. Some say
it might be that Hell is cast into a star and suggest that is what
the lake of fire is. Others suggest that this is a place beyond the
outer darkness. It could be that the lake of fire is a spiritual location superseding all comprehension for human capacity. The term
"second death" may allude to the *second level* of existence, removed
from the spiritual realm of Heaven and Hell—twice removed from
this natural plane we live on. Another concept, in the realm of
possibility, is that the term *second death* is referring to the second
level of removal from God. When considering a biblical studies
term known as the law of first mention, we see that the first time
death is referenced is in regard to the tree in the Garden of Eden.
When Adam and Eve disobeyed God, they died. These two did not
collapse and die; rather, they were removed from the Garden and
experienced a separation from God. So, death could be understood
in these terms as a separation from God. Jesus came and bridged
this gap and even reconciled man back to God.

In John 20:22, Jesus breathed on the disciples and said, "Receive
the Holy Spirit"—an act that God the Father did in Genesis when
breathing life into Adam. Jesus was reconnecting man to God; He

breathed life into them. So new life or salvation is also coming back from the dead with God. Lost people today are dead spiritually. They are separated from the Father God. If they die in that state, they will face death in eternity, and the first level is Hell. The second death, being the lake of fire, is to be twice removed from God the Father. Such a concept really could be referring to being two dimensions, two realities, two levels of judgment, or two deaths away from the One true living God.

> *For I will be merciful to their unrighteousness, and their sins and their lawless deeds I will remember no more.*
>
> **—Hebrews 8:12**

> *He will again have compassion on us, and will subdue our iniquities. You will cast all our sins into the depths of the sea.*
>
> **—Micah 7:19**

In God's infinite mercy, could it also be that just as He *remembers our sin no more*, could it be that there will be very little memory of such a place as the lake of fire and those in it in eternity future? Any conclusion we might arrive at is conjecture at best. However, what we do know is that the reality of such a place is so terrible we are not able to ascertain it. Knowing about Hell is awful enough, but it's likely we could not grasp what the second death truly is as it relates to the lake of fire.

Hell in all its fury, the lake of fire raging forever and ever, is still not enough to pay for the crime against God's holiness. If you want to understand how holy and pure God is, then consider how horrible Hell and the lake of fire are. Yet, even with all the punishment they can muster, there still isn't enough to pay for the violation against God's amazing holiness. So, God made a way for mankind to escape, through Jesus. Some might ask, "Why not the Devil and his fallen angels too? Why can't they have an opportunity to escape?" The reason is, they never had a tempter. Adam and Eve did.

On another note, angels and celestial beings are spirits, and as such they cannot be destroyed. They will exist forever somewhere.

God, who knew the horrors that would await all who would not choose Him, went through the highest extremes to get us—He sent Jesus. God preferred to give mankind the choice of accepting Him or rejecting Him, as an alternative to intentionally destroying Adam and Eve. Choice was presented to all creation rather than God intentionally leaving His son and daughter in the clutches of the Devil for all eternity. What a thought! God chose to give all humanity the choice to be with Him or live eternally separated forever, rather than permanently lose his first children by His own choice.

HOPE AND SALVATION THROUGH JESUS

There is good news—we do not have to ever experience any of the terrible things we just read about regarding a crisis eternity! As a matter of fact, God desires each person to come to Him and avoid this horrible situation altogether. It is simple to run to our Creator. First of all, know this: *God loves you!* Jesus came to seek and save all who are lost or on their way to a crisis eternity. Let me tell you how to receive Him and step into eternal life that can start right now, today!

PRAY THIS PRAYER TO RECEIVE JESUS

Jesus, I believe You are the Son of God, that You died on the cross to rescue me from sin and an eternity apart from God. I believe God raised You from the dead. I believe You came to restore me to God the Father. I repent and choose to turn away from my sins. I give myself to You, trading my life for Your life. I receive Your forgiveness and ask You to become my Savior. Wash me by Your blood. I receive You completely! I declare Jesus is my Lord! Thank You, Lord. In Jesus' name, I pray. Amen.

If you prayed this prayer or helped someone else pray it, please contact our ministry and we will send you free teaching about salvation! *Welcome to the family!*

CHAPTER TWELVE QUESTIONS

1. Why was Hell created when Satan rebelled?

_____

_____

_____

_____

_____

_____

2. What do you think about the phrase, "Sin is spiritual"?

_____

_____

_____

_____

_____

_____

3. Why does Hell last forever?

_____

_____

_____

_____

_____

_____

4. Why do you think that people preach "Hell is not eternal"?

_____

_____

_____

_____

_____

_____

5. Do you think it's possible that we will not remember those who are not in Heaven? Why?

_____

_____

_____

_____

_____

_____

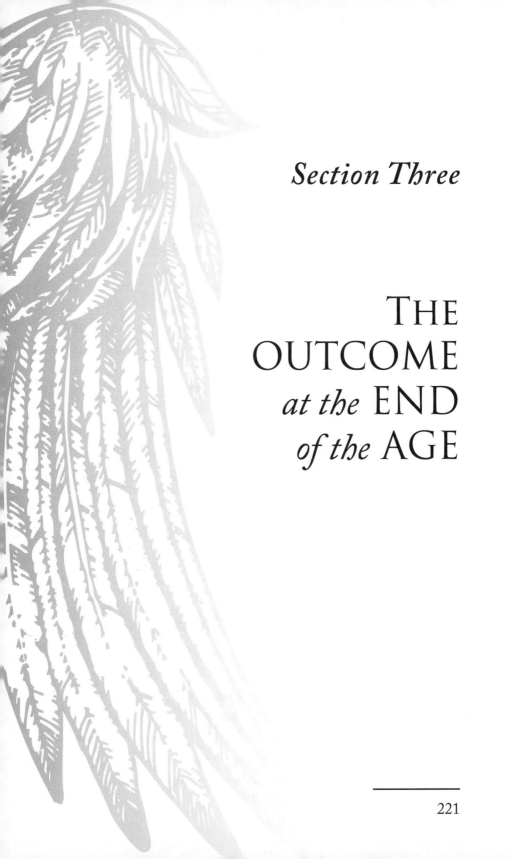

Section Three

THE
OUTCOME
at the END
of the AGE

Chapter Thirteen

THINGS ANGELS DESIRE
to INVESTIGATE

To them it was revealed that, not to themselves, but to us they
were ministering the things which now have been reported to you
through those who have preached the gospel to you by the Holy
Spirit sent from heaven—things which angels desire to look into.

1 Peter 1:12

CHERUBIM AND THE ARK

After all the magnificent things God planned in eternity
past, Jesus was now crafting the universe as the voice of
God, and the time came for the creation of man. The first
man, Adam, was a direct creation of the Father. However, Adam's
children were not direct creations of God, and the angels witnessed
this. This is also the reason Jesus is the Last Adam—because God
was also His direct Father. Jesus had always existed in eternity past
but was now sent in the flesh. The Father worked through the Son,
who manifested everything these two envisioned in the eternity
past. Angels saw this new direct creation of the Father through
this, and they once again witnessed God's great desire for humanity. Due to God's great love and desire for humanity, there is a

curiosity or "awe factor" that angels possess. We read about this in 1 Peter 1:12, which mentions, "Things which angels desire to look into." What this is referencing is everything involving mankind's relationship with God.

Angels have an interest in the affairs of mankind, especially as they relate to the gospel. The statement "things which angels desire to look into" is brought into even more light when we read how the *Latin Vulgate* references this same passage, using the wording "into whom," meaning either into the Holy Spirit and the things of the Spirit testified in the prophets and written by the apostles, or else into Christ—His person, offices, and grace.

Again, the statement "things which angels desire to look into" is also an allusion to the cherubim on the mercy seat, with the ark being a type of Christ. The cherubim looked at one another over the mercy seat with wing tips touching.

> *And the cherubim shall stretch out their wings above, covering the mercy seat with their wings, and they shall face one another; the faces of the cherubim shall be toward the mercy seat.*
>
> **—Exodus 25:20**

We might say that what was a shadow of things to come for angels was seen in the *typology* of these golden cherubim looking at the mercy seat.

JESUS THE MERCY SEAT

These angels overlooking the ark represented the angels that would one day see Jesus, who was the manifestation of what they gazed at *symbolically* on top of the ark. Additionally, angels would one day ascend and descend on the actual *Mercy Seat*, which is Jesus, the Son of Man. John 1:51 says, "And He said to him, 'Most assuredly, I say to you, hereafter you shall see heaven open, and the angels of God ascending and descending upon the Son of Man.'"

The fulfillment of angels gazing on the mercy seat again happened when Jesus rose from the dead and went to Heaven. He was seen and gazed on by angels. These *fiery servants* saw Him in the fullness of His completed assignment and experienced the fulfillment of the prophetic symbolism represented by those two cherubim positioned above the ark.

Going back again to 1 Peter 1:12, in the King James Version it mentions the phrase slightly differently, stating, "Which things the angels desire to look into." Not only was this referencing the mercy seat and Jesus being the fulfillment of that reference: "the Syriac, Arabic, and Ethiopic versions read...[as angels desiring to look into] the sufferings of Christ, and the glories following; the great mystery of redemption and salvation by Christ."[9]

What a profound thing the angels experienced! They witnessed more than prophetic types and shadows regarding the coming of the Messiah. They had complete insight into Jesus and all He was doing for us; they also witnessed Jesus conquer His enemies, showing them all that He was indeed Lord over death, Hell, and the grave. A game-changing moment for these servants of fire.

Unto whom it was revealed, that not unto themselves, but unto us they did minister the things, which are now reported unto you by them that have preached the gospel unto you with the Holy Ghost sent down from heaven; **which things** *the angels desire to look into.*

—1 Peter 1:12 KJV

And without controversy great is the mystery of godliness: God was manifested in the flesh, justified in the Spirit, **seen by angels***, preached among the Gentiles, believed on in the world, received up in glory.*

—1 Timothy 3:16

A PUBLIC SPECTACLE OF THEM

Angels desired to investigate everything that Jesus was to perform and accomplish. Another thought regarding the phrase "seen by angels" may very well be a reference to angels recognizing that they had *chosen wisely* by staying with God the Father and Jesus the Son. All He had accomplished through coming in the flesh and the work He accomplished in the Spirit was seen by angels. This is further understood in Colossians 2:15, where it reads, "He made a public spectacle of them."

Having wiped out the handwriting of requirements that was against us, which was contrary to us. And He has taken it out of the way, having nailed it to the cross.

Having disarmed principalities and powers, **He made a public spectacle of them**, *triumphing over them in it.*

—Colossians 2:14-15

The angels witnessing what Jesus had accomplished must have thought or even said to one another, "We chose wisely, boys, look at what He is doing to the ones who rebelled! That could have been us had we not chosen wisely." Being made a *public spectacle* was not only a picture of Jesus showing His victory with a celebration following, but it also showed the severity of the vengeance of the Lord. Vengeance against His enemies for destroying His creation, vengeance on behalf of all those led into darkness. This was a celebration—and it was dreadful. Why? Because real love has *hate* attached to it. God is *love*, and that comes with hatred for evil.

When the God kind of hate is understood, it is terrifying. Not to the believer but to the unbeliever who rejects God and dark powers who violated God's holy domain in the beginning. Now, many people and demonic powers carry hatred; the Devil has hatred, demonic entities carry hatred, and even wicked individuals may display hatred, but there is no comparison to the One true living God releasing hatred or anger. Hebrews gives us some insight into this part of His character.

For we know Him who said, "Vengeance is Mine, I will repay," says the Lord. And again, "The Lord will judge His people." It is a fearful thing to fall into the hands of the living God.

—Hebrews 10:30-31

> *Then He said to the disciples, "It is impossible that no*
> *offenses should come, but woe to him through whom they*
> *do come! It would be better for him if a millstone were*
> *hung around his neck, and he were thrown into the sea,*
> *than that he should offend one of these little ones."*
>
> —Luke 17:1-2

The above scripture, Luke 17:1-2, coupled with Hebrews 10:30-31 shows us a glimpse into a part of God's character as it pertains to what He hates. We know, at least in part, that God's hatred is tied directly to defending His people. For example, Revelation 2:6 says, "But this you have, that you hate the deeds of the Nicolaitans, which I also hate." This reference shows us that God hates the deeds of the Nicolaitans. For good reason—the destructive deeds of the Nicolaitans were being introduced to the church and even being taught as doctrine. An ushering in of a false belief system based on immorality and dominance over God's people was behind the perverted teaching of the Nicolaitans. God hated the deeds and persuasion of the Nicolaitans because He hates anything that hurts His family.

Dear reader, if you are in Christ Jesus, you are His building. *Building* is a term used to describe the Body of Christ, and God hates anything that tries to destroy what He loves—His people. Anyone who intentionally tries to destroy God's building, God will destroy (see 1 Corinthians 3:16-17).

ANGELS SAW JESUS IN A NEW WAY

Throughout the Old Testament, there were battles in which angels assisted the armies who were in covenant with God, and He assisted them in natural engagements. When Jesus conquered death, Hell, and the grave, followed by Him making a public spectacle of His fallen enemies, it was a *first* for the angelic ranks. They had never witnessed God working through Jesus, the Word made flesh, now punishing fallen angels and the ranks of darkness. Jesus stood as Lord of Earth and Lord in the realm of the spirit. He legally smashed what darkness had set up for thousands of years. I'm certain that these faithful angels were somber as they considered this moment. It likely induced reverence for the Lord.

Sure, they were celebrating His victory, but it must have left them with a sense of *fear* regarding what the great God of the universe was capable of. As they watched these events, the angels loyal to the Lord might have even said to one another, "We could have been with the Devil and his angels, experiencing the horrors of their disobedience. Had we gone along with their coup, we would be made a *spectacle*, just as they are, in the sight of all witnesses in the realm of the spirit!"

Every spiritual being, great or small, understood at this moment the severity for those who rebelled and declared war on God. A clear realization was now easy to comprehend—that for these fallen rebellious ones it was far too late. Punishment is all they had to look forward to. Jesus making an open display of them was only the beginning.

ENEMIES PARADED THROUGH THE STREETS

The terminology "public spectacle" from Colossians 2:14-15 is a language used in early history depicting the defeat of one kingdom by another. It was a practice of the Romans when they exposed their captives and the spoils of the conquered enemies to public view in their triumphal processions. What was often done was to parade the defeated kings and dignitaries through the streets. This is an allusion to the victories, spoils, and triumphs of the Roman emperors. When they had obtained a victory, a triumph was decreed for them by the senate. The emperor was drawn in an open chariot and the captives, stripped of their armor, had their hands tied behind them and were led before him exposed to public view and disgrace while the people shouted and cheered as he went through the city of Rome and had all the marks of honor and respect given him. Even more extreme, some believe the captives were rendered naked, their eyes gouged out, and their thumbs and big toes were cut off.

Regardless, these evil powers that had ruled over humanity with no reprieve were now at a humiliating end. Quite the statement was made through this practice, and that is exactly what Jesus was doing—making a *permanent statement*. If the more brutal side of parading the enemies through the streets has any validity, it would mean that these enemies were completely exposed. Additionally, they would never see again, walk right again, or properly hold a weapon ever again. It was in this state that these defeated foes would be on display, taken through the streets of the victorious city.

In the realm of the spirit, this played out equal to the severity of these kings and opponents put on display by the cruelty of the Romans. A moment of pure humiliation and degradation is what these enemies of Jesus were subjected to.

Those angels who were on the right side of the victorious King stood watching, highly thankful they were not suffering alongside those who defied the living God. Humiliation of the highest order is what this represents, and this is exactly what Jesus did to His adversaries. He defeated them at the crucifixion and resurrection!

Angels who had any reservations about who they should serve were now *certain* they made the correct decision as they witnessed the King of glory standing as *champion* over His adversaries.

> *To the intent that now the manifold wisdom of God might be made known by the church to the principalities and powers in the heavenly places.*
>
> —Ephesians 3:10

These ancient, rebellious foes experienced part one in the saga of their defeat. Next would come the *Ekklesia*, part two of recovering what the enemy had stolen. The Body of Christ would take authority on the Earth and defeat the kingdom of darkness until the final judgment. After Jesus was resurrected from the dead, the Church was born (see Acts 2).

It is the desire of God for the principalities and powers to know His manifold wisdom by the Church. As His Body, Jesus has empowered the Church to take dominion and educate darkness by demonstrating God's manifold wisdom in front of these principalities and powers. This will continue until the end times. Currently, we are living in the last days and have been since Acts 2. However, we are closer than ever before to the very end of the age. When the time of the Church is over, there will be a time when the Devil and his wicked horde will encounter the second death, *the lake of fire*, the final home for these nefarious creatures, forever.

After Jesus' glorious resurrection served defeat to the powers of darkness and put them on display came the empowerment of the *Ekklesia*, the Church of Jesus. God, in His wisdom, sent His Son to be a prototype for what we are to collectively be. Not only did Jesus defeat the powers of darkness, but He also wants us to enforce what

He accomplished. Today, we have authority over snakes, scorpions, and all the power of the enemy. In part this is to finish what He purposed with the gospel, as well as prepare His Body to rule in *eternity future* as kings and lords. You might say that this life is a one-shot dress rehearsal for eternity. How you deal with opposition from the enemy is practice. How any believer overcomes during this present evil age is a proving ground for what lies ahead.

Jesus our Lord—our great High Priest, the author and finisher of our faith—has shown us how winning is done. A kingdom of darkness remains, although defeated; we are to enforce the victory provided for us and continue to transfer anyone and everyone we can into the kingdom of God. The Devil knows his time is short, that his days are numbered. As the Body of Christ, we are in a race to win as many as we can, before the coming of the great and terrible day of the Lord, when He will finally sentence and execute the full force of the destined punishment on all darkness. It is not a mystery to any Bible-believing person that this day will come. Your job is to rise up, overcome, make disciples, and recognize you have been given the authority to stand against the wickedness induced from the very beginning by Lucifer.

CHAPTER THIRTEEN QUESTIONS

1. Why do you think angels have an interest in the affairs of mankind?

_____

_____

_____

_____

_____

_____

2. What is the connection between Jesus and the mercy seat and the angels on the ark of the covenant?

_____

_____

_____

_____

_____

_____

3. Why do you think the angels that didn't rebel against God
   were grateful for their eternal decision compared to those that
   did rebel?

_____

_____

_____

_____

_____

_____

Chapter Fourteen

FOREVER ALLEGIANCE
to the LAMB *of* GOD

For behold, I create new heavens and a new earth; and
the former shall not be remembered or come to mind.
Isaiah 65:17

Then he said to me, "Write: 'Blessed are those who are called to
the marriage supper of the Lamb!'" And he said to me, "These are
the true sayings of God." And I fell at his feet to worship him.
But he said to me, "See that you do not do that! I am your fellow
servant, and of your brethren who have the testimony of Jesus.
Worship God! For the testimony of Jesus is the spirit of prophecy."
Revelation 19:9-10

John had a tremendous encounter with a servant of fire—an encounter so overwhelming that John fell to his face and began to worship. Circumstances such as this make it understandable why John would fall down to his face to worship. Imagine being in this position! Here is a man who knew Jesus from a young age; he was a major leader in the Body of Christ, and an all-encompassing spiritual unveiling was being shared with him in supernatural wave after wave. John could barely take it! Finally, he broke by falling down to worship. In this brief moment, it is not the act of falling down that I would like you to notice; rather, it is the response of the angel!

Upon bowing down and nearly engaging in a state of worship, the angel abruptly stopped John. "See that you do not do that!" the angel said with intensity. It wasn't that the angel was upset with John—no, this angel knew he had another audience. The great God of the universe was watching, and at this moment I believe the angel had flashbacks, like a war veteran who had witnessed battles no civilian would understand. Memories and trauma filled the remembrance of this angel. The stress of this moment was not directed at John. No, the stress of this moment was the result of an archangel who demanded to be worshiped by mankind and, if possible, even the Son of God! This angel was having none of it! "See that you do not do that!" was the knee-jerk reaction of a war veteran, a survivor who knew more than a man like John could ever comprehend. This reaction was from someone who witnessed the outcome of a nefarious coup that left Heaven scarred.

It is fascinating to discover that upon deeper consideration of this moment you might begin to realize that this alludes to mankind's rank in creation. For a man to worship any angel is to find themselves in a lower position than they were created for. In 1 Corinthians 6:3, Paul says, "Do you not know that we shall judge angels?" Here we see John falling before a being that was beneath him! He was reminded sternly, "Worship God!" pleaded the angel. No fallen angel nor any other created thing is worthy to be worshiped! Another reason this angel stopped the prophet from worshiping was (as you read a moment ago) that God was watching.

Letting God know he was a loyal servant was imperative at this moment. It was the very action Lucifer wanted.

> *For you have said in your heart: "I will ascend into heaven, I will exalt my throne above the stars of God; I will also sit on the mount of the congregation on the farthest sides of the north; I will ascend above the heights of the clouds, I will be like the Most High."*
>
> —Isaiah 14:13-14

Everything has an origin. In the case of all things stealing, killing, and destroying, the origin is found in Lucifer, who ultimately became Satan.

> *Thou art the anointed cherub that covereth; and I have set thee so: thou wast upon the holy mountain of God; thou hast walked up and down in the midst of the stones of fire. Thou wast perfect in thy ways from the day that thou wast created, till* **iniquity was found in thee. By the multitude of thy merchandise they have filled the midst of thee with violence,** *and thou hast sinned: therefore I will cast thee as profane out of the mountain of God: and I will destroy thee, O covering cherub, from the midst of the stones of fire. Thine heart was lifted up because of thy beauty, thou hast corrupted thy wisdom by reason of thy brightness: I will cast thee to the ground, I will lay thee before kings, that they may behold thee. Thou hast defiled thy sanctuaries by the multitude of thine iniquities, by the iniquity of thy traffick; therefore will I bring forth a fire from the midst of thee, it shall devour thee, and I will*

bring thee to ashes upon the earth in the sight of all them that behold thee. All they that know thee among the people shall be astonished at thee: thou shalt be a terror, and never shalt thou be any more.

—Ezekiel 28:14-19 KJV

The above passage of Scripture is the story arc of Lucifer turned Satan from the days of his radiance to his imminent punishment. There are many fascinating pieces within the journey of this fallen cherub. Certainly, he was once a beautiful angel, and he potentially was the worship leader in Heaven, having full access to God's creation. Verse 14 speaks of him walking up and down in the midst of the stones of fire, which is likely a reference to the planets in our solar system. He had access to everything on and around the Earth, both in the natural realm and the spirit realm. God created him perfectly in all his ways until the day he decided to indulge in iniquity. This was due to jealousy toward God.

THE DEVIL'S TANTRUM

Job 4 gives insight into the Devil's contempt for God and the Devil's hatred toward mankind. Eliphaz, one of Job's friends, is within earshot of a rhetorical conversation the Devil is having with himself. This leads to Eliphaz involuntarily eavesdropping on the moment.

Now a word was secretly brought to me, and my ear received a whisper of it. In disquieting thoughts from the visions of the night, when deep sleep falls on men, fear came upon me, and trembling, which made all my bones shake. Then a spirit passed before my face; the hair on my body stood up. It stood still, but I could not discern its appearance. A form was before my eyes; there was silence; then I heard a voice saying: "Can a mortal be more righteous than God? Can a man be more pure than his Maker? If He puts no trust in His servants, if He charges His angels with error, how much more those who dwell in houses of clay, whose foundation is in the dust, who are crushed before a moth? They are broken in pieces from morning till evening; they perish forever, with no one regarding. Does not their own excellence go away? They die, even without wisdom."

—Job 4:12-21

Eliphaz sensed the presence of the fallen angel, and the encounter was a terrifying scenario that induced trembling, bones shaking, and the hair on his body stood up. In this same moment, he could identify a formless entity before his eyes, until finally a voice spoke.

If Eliphaz could have seen past all the theatrics—meaning the fear, darkness, and sense of dread—what is left is a voice that begins to complain to itself! About God, no less! A voice that sounds like the tantrum of a six-year-old. This scenario is a strange moment experienced by Eliphaz as he was eavesdropping on the Devil, who was whining and telling himself that he is so much better than humans.

This unique story shows us that the Devil never got over being outranked by dirt. This tantrum gives insight into his self-pity and contempt for mankind and God.

Eliphaz's encounter gives us insight into Satan's disdain for humanity and contempt for God, which led to an insatiable desire to rule the world. His hatred for mankind comes from the reality that God placed mankind in a higher position than him! We are in the place Lucifer desired to be. He desired that all humanity be under him in a debased fashion. This same issue involved the economy of the world, some believe, before the time of Adam!

Ezekiel 28:16 (KJV) gives insight into what the Devil was doing in a time frame well before the days we live in. It reads, "By *the multitude of thy merchandise* they have filled the midst of thee with violence." The Amplified Bible says it this way, "Through *the abundance of your commerce* you were internally filled with lawlessness and violence, and you sinned."

There was a point when the Devil had an abundance of commerce on Earth. The full meaning of this is not clear. One thing we know, it involved what was potentially an ancient global economy on a large scale. The Devil has always wanted to dominate mankind, and the best way he could rule over the masses would be to place himself in control of the resources and economy of the entire world. This would make him the authority of men's dealings.

> *Being tempted for forty days by the devil. And in those days He ate nothing, and afterward, when they had ended, He was hungry. And the devil said to Him, "If You are the Son of God, command this stone to become bread." But Jesus answered him, saying, "It is written, 'Man shall not live by bread alone, but by every word of God.'"* **Then the devil, taking Him up on a high mountain, showed Him all the kingdoms of the world in a moment of time. And the devil said to Him, "All this authority I will give You,**

and their glory; for this has been delivered to me, and I give it to whomever I wish. Therefore, if You will worship before me, all will be Yours." And Jesus answered and said to him, "Get behind Me, Satan! For it is written, 'You shall worship the Lord your God, and Him only you shall serve.'" Then he brought Him to Jerusalem, set Him on the pinnacle of the temple, and said to Him, "If You are the Son of God, throw Yourself down from here. For it is written: 'He shall give His angels charge over you, to keep you,' and, 'In their hands they shall bear you up, lest you dash your foot against a stone.'" And Jesus answered and said to him, "It has been said, 'You shall not tempt the Lord your God.'" Now when the devil had ended every temptation, he departed from Him until an opportune time.*

—Luke 4:2-13

The Devil wasn't lying about what he had; it was indeed given to him. Many times, we read these verses and come away with the understanding that Jesus defeated the Devil three times. What the vast majority don't understand is the magnitude of what was happening here. First, we need to recognize that this was indeed a temptation for Jesus. How do we know this? Because that is what the Word of God calls it. He was tempted for forty days by the Devil. During this time, He didn't eat anything. He was likely feeling weak as His flesh was deprived of food and comfort; Jesus was in a vulnerable position. The Devil knew this and waited until the very end of the forty days to pull out all the stops. As if to say, "Let's just cut to the chase here—I can give you what you came for. Why suffer? I will hand over to you what you are seeking. The exchange is simple—just bow down and worship me."

This was not the first time the Devil used this type of ploy. It was a familiar strategy and was used previously with another son of God—the original humankind son, the first Adam. When the lying serpent deceived Eve, Adam was standing next to her. The Devil was able to convince Adam and Eve that God was withholding something from them. As a result, they believed the word of the serpent over the command of the Lord. This resulted in Adam and Eve placing their authority and dominion in the control of Satan. This becomes even clearer in the chapters of Job in which we learn that the Devil had the authority not only to appear before God with the angels but additionally had the authority to do a variety of horrible things to Job. This is because he was now operating in the authority of the first Adam.

Upon his temptation of Jesus, he said in Luke 4:6, "All this *authority* I will give You, and their *glory*; for this has been delivered to me, and I give it to whomever I wish."

- **Authority/Power:** in the original Greek language, this word represents the executive power of one's rule, dominion, domain, and jurisdiction.
- **Glory:** in the original Greek and etymologically, *glory* primarily means thought or opinion, especially favorable human opinion, reputation, praise, or honor, whether it is true or false honor.

Satan was saying to Jesus, "Not only can I give You complete executive power over every kingdom on Earth, but I can also make everyone who is a part of that system praise You and create any desired reputation for You I wish."

The issue at hand was severe, as this was a similar strategy that had worked on the first Adam. It is what gave the Devil all his executive authority over creation. Satan had grown comfortable ruling over the majority of mankind. He was unchallenged for hundreds of years, doing as he pleased, manipulating and corrupting men as he saw fit. That is, until this moment. The moment he engaged in tempting this new individual. This latest voice on the scene. Surely this one would be like all the others whom he had pressured and compromised all the way back to the garden.

Over forty days he unleashed his best persuasion, his highest level of temptation. He became more and more aware that he was dealing with someone vastly different from the first Adam and all who came afterward. The realization must have set in with a growing horror for Satan, with each failed temptation becoming clearer—he was colliding with someone who was strategically weaponized against him. The prince of this world, for the first time, was encountering a man prepared and fashioned for this very fight. This one was sent to destroy all Satan had established and all he had built for generations. Jesus came to destroy the works of the Devil (see 1 John 3:8).

Satan had entered into a confrontation with the Last Adam.

THE LAST ADAM

And so it is written, "The first man Adam became a living being." The last Adam became a life-giving spirit.
—**1 Corinthians 15:45**

Not only was the Last Adam a direct Son of God, but He was also God in the flesh, the firstborn among many brethren, a life-giving spirit. Notice the Bible doesn't refer to Him as the second Adam; no, He is the Last Adam. There was no plan B after Him.

Jesus was the last line of defense. He was God's perfect plan developed over hundreds of years to be unleashed on this rebellious, fallen angel at just the right moment. This first engagement with Jesus must have left the Devil bewildered and highly concerned. Jesus rendered his temptations to a screeching halt by authoritatively declaring, "It is written." This sent the Devil back on his heels; he had to go away and strategize when he might find another opportunity to overtake this powerful new foe. Luke 4:13 says, "Now when the devil had ended every temptation, he departed from Him until an opportune time."

The Devil must have known Jesus was different; he remembered the prophecy God Himself spoke in Genesis 3:15 (NIV), saying, "He will crush your head, and you will strike his heel." In Satan's arrogance, he decided this was his big opportunity. If Jesus was the one God had prophesied about, then it was time to make a big play, not just for dominion over the Earth—this time, for the entire kingdom of God, of Heaven, and complete dominance over mankind forever. What an unbelievable thought, that God the Father loved us so much that He gave His only Son, sacrificially, and under the risk of losing Him (as well as us forever) to the temptation of the Devil. Imagine what would have happened if Jesus bowed to the Devil. It is possible Earth, Heaven, and the kingdom of God would all fall under Satan's authority. He (Satan) would have won! We would all be eternally under the dominion of a fallen angel! He would enforce a kingdom of stealing, killing, and destroying. However, this new contender was found without blemish, without weakness; He was perfect; He came and condemned sin in the flesh. Another clearer way of saying this would be to say Jesus condemned sin on its own turf.

Jesus slapped sin and death around, then threw them all out of their own party!

Even with all that was riding on the line, Satan quickly discovered he was not dealing with the first Adam. He wasn't dealing with a typical king or corruptible man—far from it. He was dealing with someone he didn't count on; he was dealing with the Last Adam. Not a mere man, Satan was now confronted with God in the flesh, who had arrived to destroy the works of the Devil. Jesus didn't come to consider the Devil's offers or negotiate; He came to declare war on the kingdom of darkness! This realization must have enraged and terrified Satan when he offered Jesus everything He came to accomplish—minus the suffering, rejection, and difficulty that would be necessary for Jesus to endure if He was to reclaim a world that had fallen into the hands of Satan. This was the shortcut; Satan was sure Jesus would take the bait and that He would fall to His knees, rendering everything Satan's. His wicked rule would have become permanent and irrevocable. Thank God that the Devil's highest and best temptations were no match for the Son of the living God. Jesus didn't falter. He released His confession and His faith mixed with the Word of God: "It is written!"

Three times He replied to the Devil, "It is written."

It is written, *"Man shall not live by bread alone, but by every word of God."*

—Luke 4:4

And Jesus answered and said to him, "Get behind Me, Satan! For *it is written,* *'You shall worship the Lord your God, and Him only you shall serve.'"*

—Luke 4:8

*Jesus said to him, "*It is written again,* 'You shall not tempt the Lord your God.'"*

—Matthew 4:7

What the Devil was tempting Jesus with was Hell's economy and its entire system. He was offering Jesus control of the commerce that he himself possessed in an old world. He offered Jesus a reputation with the entire world and to sit as king over the Earth—of course, with the Devil seated in the place of God. The thing the Devil may not have realized was that Jesus wasn't in the Devil's arena; the Devil was now in His. Jesus had arrived to legally claim back what the Devil had taken by deception from Adam and Eve. Jesus was here to set up the kingdom of God and empower a whole new generation with His words and authority to drive the Devil and his influence out. This was a purely savage move by God the Father and Jesus the Son. He humbled Himself and became a man to have revenge on the prince of darkness and give every living person the opportunity to be free once and for all time!

Jesus was the firstborn among many brethren. He was the proto-type for how we are to treat the Devil and the kingdom of darkness and every demonic adversary. Nothing has changed; the Devil is still the author of stealing, killing, and destroying. Jesus said while addressing the Pharisees that the Devil was a murderer from the beginning and that his native tongue is lying.

> *You are of your father the devil, and the desires of your father you want to do. He was a murderer from the begin-ning, and does not stand in the truth, because there is no truth in him. When he speaks a lie, he speaks from his own resources, for he is a liar and the father of it.*
>
> —John 8:44

THE LONG-SUFFERING OF GOD

Another observation to consider may be found in the narrative of Judas. Much like Lucifer was near God the Father, Judas was near the Lord Jesus. He was His treasurer, and Judas saw all the mira-cles and everything else the other disciples witnessed. Yet, he still carried contempt in his heart. Not directly at Jesus, but it was likely that Jesus was not doing things the way Judas wanted Him to be doing them.

Some Bible scholars suggest that Judas likely believed the prophecies of the Messiah much like many of them did. However, when Jesus failed to step up and lead a revolt against Rome, the current oppressors of Israel, Judas decided to hand Jesus over to the institutional leaders, ultimately selling Him for thirty pieces of silver. Now, Jesus knew what was in Judas—He knew Judas would betray Him, and yet He allowed Judas to remain. Could it be that God is so *humble* and lowly of heart that He allowed this wrong to be done against Him? Certainly, what we do know is that the Lord loved Judas. The Lord also loved Lucifer *until iniquity was found in him.*

> *You were perfect in your ways from the day you were created, till iniquity was found in you.*
>
> —**Ezekiel 28:15**

God's love changed to a mission of destroying the works of the Devil once God's children and His direct creations became involved. It's almost as if God took major action once Lucifer turned to Satan and deceived Adam and Eve. That is when the Lord pronounced judgment upon him. Genesis 3:14-15 says, "So the Lord said to the serpent: 'Because you have done this, you are cursed more than all cattle, and more than every beast of the field; on your belly you shall go, and you shall eat dust all the days of your life. And I will put enmity between you and the woman, and between your seed and her Seed; He shall bruise your head, and you shall bruise His heel.'"

Michael fought the battle with his angels against Lucifer and his angels. However, it wasn't until humanity was threatened by what would be a *hostage situation* by the Devil that the Lord took direct action. Judas was another avenue for darkness to assault the Lord. Judas became open to the darkness. He started out as a thief of the money box and ultimately made deals with the religious leaders of the day to destroy Jesus. Ultimately, Satan entered him. What a horrible thing! Satan entered Judas!

Then Satan entered Judas, surnamed Iscariot, who was numbered among the twelve.

—**Luke 22:3**

Now after the piece of bread, Satan entered him. Then Jesus said to him, "What you do, do quickly."

—**John 13:27**

Here is the point that I'm making. If Jesus allowed Judas to be around, and Jesus is the exact representation of the Father, could it be that God the Father, knowing all things, held out as long as He could for Lucifer to do what was right? Ultimately, both Lucifer and Judas made their decision. To me, this points out the innocence of God to a remarkable level. He is pure and long-suffering, willing that no one would perish, even Lucifer in the beginning. God also has chosen to let every created being choose. Choose Him or their own way.

This same great God started out creating a world that was perfect, filled with inhabitants of perfection and everything anyone or anything could ever want. Yet, pride and selfish ambition were the downfall not only of angels but also humankind, who chose to take the serpent's word over God's Word. How sad this must have been for the living God, the innocent Creator who, despite all these events He knew would happen, still decided the opportunity for a relationship with you was worth it all! He is amazing!

CHAPTER FOURTEEN QUESTIONS

1. Why did the angel in Revelation immediately stop John from worshiping him?

_____

_____

_____

_____

2. How did Jesus overcome the Devil when He was tempted in the wilderness?

_____

_____

_____

_____

3. What does it mean that Jesus is the Last Adam?

_____

_____

_____

_____

Chapter Fifteen

ETERNAL COMPANIONS
for REIGNING

And there shall be no more curse: but the throne of God and of the
Lamb shall be in it; and his servants shall serve him: and they shall
see his face; and his name shall be in their foreheads. And there shall
be no night there; and they need no candle, neither light of the sun; for
the Lord God giveth them light: and they shall reign for ever and ever.
Revelation 22:3-5 KJV

Eternity future is a subject we have limited information about, but it is something to consider. This is because the vast majority of every person's existence will be lived out forever in the eons of eternity future. A glimpse of this is found in Revelation 22:5 (KJV), which reads, "They shall reign for ever and ever." This is a statement regarding the kings and lords who are simply believers in eternity future.

Adam and Eve were most likely going to continue expanding their responsibility into the universe. The Tower of Babel might have been a perversion of man's desire to go beyond what we know in our natural world. Additionally, consider mankind's interest in early expeditions or space exploration. We have the desire to expand, study, and develop. Could it be that this internal desire to know more about the great beyond is a piece within that still wants to be fulfilled? A missing element of reaching past the known and attaining knowledge of the unknown? We might be stepping into the future of why God created the universe in the first place—for His children to occupy and develop it! Of course, this is all speculation and conjecture, yet it is a real consideration. Something we do know is that God will create a new Heaven and a new Earth.

> *Now I saw a new heaven and a new earth, for the first heaven and the first earth had passed away. Also there was no more sea.*
>
> **—Revelation 21:1**

> *And have made us kings and priests to our God; and we shall reign on the earth.*
>
> **—Revelation 5:10**

It might come as a surprise to some that humanity was not created to live in Heaven. It's true, we were created in the beginning to live on the Earth and take dominion over it. Revelation 21:1 says there will be a new Earth. It is in the realm of possibility that the new Earth will be a staging ground for the kings and lords to rule and reign.

KINGS AND LORDS

And He has on His robe and on His thigh a name written: KING OF KINGS AND LORD OF LORDS.

—Revelation 19:16

Kings and lords both do something—they rule over territory. Now, notice it says that Jesus is the *King of kings* and *Lord of lords*. Jesus has the name above all names, and everything and everyone will be under His complete reign and authority. It is likely that His people who lived for Him in this life will be awarded rule and responsibility in the age to come.

How are rules and responsibilities determined? By faithfulness here in this age. Let's look at the parable of minas as it sheds light on the concept of faithfulness and rewards.

*Therefore He said: "A certain nobleman went into a far country to receive for himself a kingdom and to return. So he called **ten of his servants**, delivered to them ten minas, and said to them, 'Do business till I come.' But his citizens hated him, and sent a delegation after him, saying, 'We will not have this man to reign over us.'*

*"And so it was that when he returned, having received the kingdom, he then commanded these servants, to whom he had given the money, to be called to him, that he might know how much every man had gained by trading. Then came the first, saying, '**Master, your mina has earned ten minas.**' And he said to him, '**Well done, good servant; because you were faithful in a very little, have***

authority over ten cities.' And the second came, saying, *'Master, your mina has earned **five minas.'** Likewise he said to him, 'You also be over **five cities.'***

"Then another came, saying, 'Master, here is your mina, which I have kept put away in a handkerchief. For I feared you, because you are an austere man. You collect what you did not deposit, and reap what you did not sow.' And he said to him, 'Out of your own mouth I will judge you, you wicked servant. You knew that I was an austere man, collecting what I did not deposit and reaping what I did not sow. Why then did you not put my money in the bank, that at my coming I might have collected it with interest?'

"And he said to those who stood by, 'Take the mina from him, and give it to him who has ten minas.' (But they said to him, 'Master, he has ten minas.') 'For I say to you, that to everyone who has will be given; and from him who does not have, even what he has will be taken away from him. But bring here those enemies of mine, who did not want me to reign over them, and slay them before me.'"

—Luke 19:12-27

Notice the comparison of faithfulness with minas and how it translated to cities! What the stewards did with the amount they were given was equivalent to the level of cities they would have authority over. This parable holds truth that may give us insight into how the eternity future might look. What we do here in this time with what we have been entrusted to steward is the metric we will be rewarded by. This is a sobering truth, not to be taken lightly. Pay attention to what the reward is—authority over a territory. Jesus is the *King of kings* ruling over territories. This is a governmental position. In eternity future our faithfulness will be a determining factor in the territory that we will rule over as kings.

YOU WILL JUDGE ANGELS

> *Do you not know that the saints will judge the world? And if the world will be judged by you, are you unworthy to judge the smallest matters? Do you not know that we shall judge angels? How much more, things that pertain to this life?*
>
> —1 Corinthians 6:2-3

Saints judging the world carries a powerful understanding and completes a full circle reaching all the way back to Adam's dominion. When Jesus returned Adam's executive privilege to the people of God, it gave them the ability to exercise kingdom authority on earth during this current age. In the age to come, this authority will increase. The Greek word for *judge* is *krino* and means to make a legal decision. It does not refer to directly passing sentences on angels or sending them to eternal punishment. However, it does imply that saints will be exalted higher than angels, will rule in a class above them, and will carry authority to make administrative decisions in eternity future. More than likely, saints will witness and approve the sentencing of angels by the living God.

In many Jewish traditions, one of the things taught was that the righteous would judge the nations. This judging could also imply judging angels who were believed to *rule* the nations they were assigned to. Although this is no more than a tradition and not what the Bible teaches plainly, it does bring up an interesting point of speculation. Might angels be held accountable in a similar way to believers? If believers are to give an accounting for what they were entrusted, such as was the case in the parable of the minas, could a similar accounting be issued for the celestial hierarchies responsible for nations, cities, and territories? There is no absolute conclusion, but it is a point of interest.

FIERY COMPANIONS

Jesus is the great King over many kings, and He is also the firstborn among many brethren. The eternal reign of King Jesus will be a universal reign. Those who have followed Him will likely be sent out and positioned with a governmental authority over territories and regions.

Accompanying the kings and lords in eternity will be the continuation of the servants of fire. After all, this is their *mission* today. Why would it cease once we are in the age to come?

Angels will assist in the continuation of what the Lord gave Adam authority for—to take dominion, tend the garden, and grow. It was possibly God's plan from the beginning that Adam would expand to the entire Earth and eventually tend to other planets. Now, this can't be proven, but it is an interesting thought, especially when considering the rocky planets we can view and measure that have no life on them. Who is to say that once we arrive at the age of a new Heaven and new Earth, we will not begin establishing the lordship of Jesus to the farthest reaches of the universe? Whatever it might be that you are given authority over, it is wonderful to realize that the *servants of fire* will be present in a working relationship for the building of God's kingdom throughout eternity future!

CHAPTER FIFTEEN QUESTIONS

1. What do you think awaits believers in eternity future?

_____

_____

_____

_____

2. How might responsibilities in eternity future be determined among kings and lords?

_____

_____

_____

_____

3. How will we "judge" angels?

_____

_____

_____

_____

_____

_____

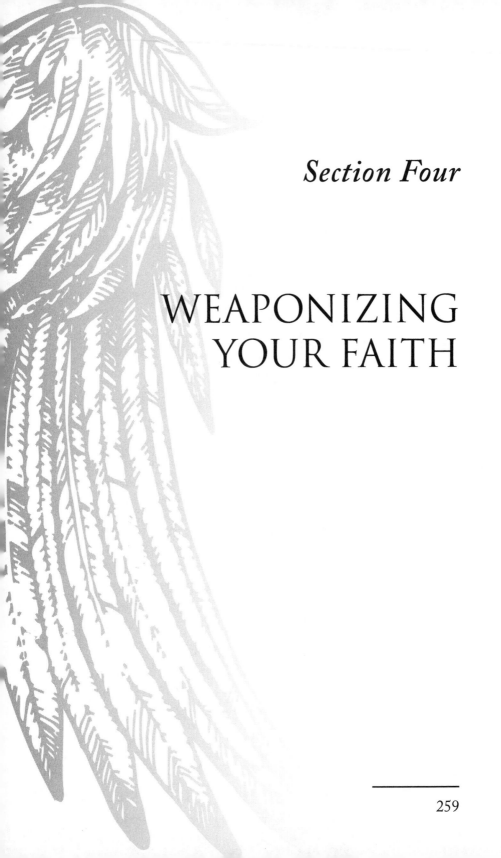

Section Four

WEAPONIZING YOUR FAITH

SERVANTS OF FIRE
PRAYER GUIDE

At the beginning of your supplications the command went out,
and I have come to tell you, for you are greatly beloved.

Daniel 9:23

This section on prayer, and even more specifically where it refers to prayers that release angels, is a selection of notes I have assembled. My family and I use these notes often when we pray together.

According to the Word of God, how a person prays has the potential to greatly unlock angelic activity. It is my desire to see you thrive with assistance from the armies of Heaven bringing aid, protection, and provision, and working on your behalf regarding things you are not even aware of.

Because of our covenant with God the Father through the blood of Jesus, we have the wonderful privilege to enforce His will on this Earth. One of the ways we do so is to pray His Word. If you ever wonder what the will of God is, just pray out His Word over any situation, and you will know what His will is concerning the matter at hand.

For example, when facing any type of difficulty, pray out John 10:10, which says, "The thief does not come except to steal, and to kill, and to destroy. I have come that they may have life, and that they may have it more abundantly."

You could pray this way, "Lord, I know the difficulty I'm facing is not from You, for it is the enemy who comes to steal, kill, and destroy. I see in Your Word that You have come to give me life, and to give it more abundantly. So right now in Jesus' name, I agree with Your Word over me for abundant life! By faith, I receive an abundance of life, and the God quality of life right now in the name of Jesus!"

When facing challenges regarding the world around you and all the pressures of society, you could read this scripture and pray.

> *Who gave Himself for our sins, that He might deliver us from this present evil age, according to the will of our God and Father.*

> **—Galatians 1:4**

Here is a prayer to pray with this scripture:

Lord, I thank You that it is Your will that I will be delivered from this present evil age. So right now, I line up with Your will for my life and declare deliverance from every evil thing in this present time. In Jesus' mighty name!

You can go on praying by declaring:

> Since it is Your will that I be delivered from this present evil age, then I declare all emotional oppression must go! I declare all anxiety must leave me now! I receive everything that is the opposite of this present evil age. I receive favor, blessing, increase, health, good family, right relationships, purpose, and any other thing that lines up with the goodness of God.

AVOIDING VAIN REPETITIONS

And when you pray, do not use vain repetitions as the heathen do. For they think that they will be heard for their many words. Therefore do not be like them. For your Father knows the things you have need of before you ask Him.

—Matthew 6:7-8

It is important to get past religious praying. One of the main culprits is vain repetitions. This type of praying is simply a religious form of praying that involves repetition and using a lot of words. Jesus referred to vain repetition, comparing it to how *heathens* pray. The statement Jesus made, "they think they will be heard for their many words," is basically saying that some people put more faith in the length of their prayers rather than in God.

Religion has everything to do with God—but our hearts.

Religion has everything to do with God—but our hearts. Let me explain. Religion is doing all the right things, looking the part, acting the part, or even doing everything right in form and for the eyes of everyone else. However, it is not truly connected to God. Why? Because religion is a human doing and trying to achieve something to please God. Religion is not a heart conversion; it is an outward act without a connection on the inside. Our heart refers to the soulish arena and comprises our mind, will, and emotions. Without having a true heart connection to God by His Word, we are practicing religion, not a relationship. For years I have made the statement that religion has everything to do with God—but our hearts. The same could be said about prayer. Without hearts full of faith and a connection to the Lord, prayer can also become a formality, which counteracts actual results.

Here is an example: going back to Matthew 6:8, Jesus said, "Do not be like them." In context, He had just finished speaking about the Pharisees and giving the example of how they would pray loudly to be seen by men, along with the other hypocritical ways they would parade themselves for religious applause. Vain repetition is not faith-filled, relationship-based praying; rather, it is badgering and transactional. Our God is not a head God, He is a heart God. Religion and all other forms of praying to gain results without God's prescription are in themselves vain. God wants your heart and has given us a biblical understanding to know how we ought to pray so that it is effective. However, the heart alone is not enough either. The world we live in has spiritual laws in motion, and the purpose of knowing how to pray is for meeting the requirements for abiding by spiritual laws. Another way of saying this would be that there are protocols for effectiveness.

In Chapter One we saw four types of prayer as listed in 1 Timothy 2:1:

1. Supplications

2. Prayers

3. Intercessions

4. Giving thanks

Another area that should be mentioned is the area of speaking to obstacles.

> *So Jesus answered and said to them, "Have faith in God. For assuredly, I say to you, whoever* **says** *to this mountain, 'Be removed and be cast into the sea,' and* **does not doubt in his heart, but believes that those things he says will be done, he will have whatever he says.** *Therefore I say to you,* **whatever things you ask when you pray, believe that you receive them, and you will have them.** *And whenever you stand praying, if you have anything against anyone, forgive him, that your Father in heaven may also forgive you your trespasses. But if you do not forgive, neither will your Father in heaven forgive your trespasses."*
> —**Mark 11:22-26**

Jesus said:

1. Have faith in God.

2. Speak to the mountain or issue you are facing.

3. Do not doubt but believe.

4. You will have what you say!

5. Finally, walk in forgiveness toward everyone.

What weapons Jesus told us about! He wants us to exercise these for effective living.

> *The effective, fervent prayer of a righteous man avails much.*
>
> —James 5:16

The righteous man should be armed with effective praying. Effective means they know how to pray properly, but notice it says *fervently*. As we learned in Chapter One, this word *fervently* means to put forth power, to be at work, or be self-operative. When you know how to pray and exercise it fervently, you will accomplish much!

SCRIPTURAL PRAYERS THAT AUTHORIZE ANGELS

Now, the main purpose of this section is to pray scriptures that authorize and release angelic activity God's way, not man's way. Below is a list of scriptures I use in my prayer life. After several days of reading these and praying them out, an angelic encounter took place with my wife and me in our home. I listed these as it has been a source of effectiveness in our lives, and it is our prayer that it will be in yours.

THE REALM OF THE UNSEEN IS GREATER

I share the below scriptures to remind you that the realm of the unseen is powerful. Much like Elisha's servant, it is easy to get our eyes on the natural world, but if we could see what was happening behind the veil, I believe the response would be much like the servant! Keep this in mind as we step into releasing the armies of Heaven through prayer.

> And when the servant of the man of God arose early and went out, there was an army, surrounding the city with horses and chariots. And his servant said to him, "Alas, my master! What shall we do?" So he answered, "Do not fear, for those who are with us are more than those who are with them." And Elisha prayed, and said, "Lord, I pray, open his eyes that he may see." Then the Lord opened the eyes of the young man, and he saw. And behold, **the mountain was full of horses and chariots of fire all around Elisha.** So when the Syrians came down to him, Elisha prayed to the Lord, and said, "Strike this people, I pray, with blindness." And He struck them with blindness according to the word of Elisha.
>
> —2 Kings 6:15-18

SCRIPTURAL DECLARATIONS

And of the angels He says: "Who makes His angels spirits and His ministers a flame of fire."

—Hebrews 1:7

*Are they not all **ministering spirits sent forth to minister for those who will inherit salvation?***

—Hebrews 1:14

Lord, I thank You that You make Your angels spirits and ministering flames of fire for my sake and the sake of my loved ones.

The voice of the Lord divides the flames of fire.

—Psalm 29:7

I thank You, Lord, that when I speak any promise from Your Word (out loud) Your flames of fire are divided into ranks for assignment.

Declare a scripture promise: _____

Bless the Lord, you His angels, who excel in strength, who do His word, heeding the voice of His word. Bless the Lord, all you His hosts, you ministers of His, who do His pleasure. Bless the Lord, all His works, in all places of His dominion. Bless the Lord, O my soul!

—Psalm 103:20-22

Lord, I thank You that Your Word is alive and active in me and that I can speak Your Word and the angels will heed the voice of Your Word and respond.

Thank You that Your angels do Your pleasure for my sake and my family and that it pleases You when we speak the Word to activate angels.

Right now, in Jesus' name, I declare (insert your personal prayer) that Your servants of fire heed it and do Your pleasure over my life!

Let them shout for joy and be glad, who favor my righteous cause; and let them say continually, "Let the Lord be magnified, who has pleasure in the prosperity of His servant."

—Psalm 35:27

Thank You, Lord, that according to Psalm 103:21 angels do Your pleasure. Psalm 35:27 says You have pleasure in my prosperity. So right now, in Jesus' name, I agree with the prosperity of God over my life and that angels are being sent out to fulfill Your pleasure over me.

Behold, I send an Angel before you to keep you in the way and to bring you into the place which I have prepared.
—**Exodus 23:20**

Behold, I send an Angel before you to keep and guard you on the way and to bring you to the place I have prepared.
—**Exodus 23:20 AMPC**

This Scripture is the release of angelic preparation of where you are currently and where you are headed. Use this when praying over your life and future plans, but also use it in prayers about moving to new locations, trips, or ventures.

Thank You, Lord, that You have placed an angel before me to keep and guard me on my way to the place that You have prepared for me.

Then the Lord sent an angel who cut down every mighty man of valor, leader, and captain in the camp of the king of Assyria. So he returned shamefaced to his own land. And when he had gone into the temple of his god, some of his own offspring struck him down with the sword there.

—2 Chronicles 32:21

This is a powerful prayer scripture to use regarding stopping the attacks of the enemy over any particular situation.

Lord, I call forth Your angels to cut down every assignment, influence, or evil persuasion against You that is attacking my life. That evil plans would be cut down, the plans of darkness would fail, and that the thing fighting against me would be turned away shamefaced and sent back to where it came from.

The angel of the Lord encamps all around those who fear Him, and delivers them.

—Psalm 34:7

This is a prayer for the divine angelic protection of those who fear the Lord.

Lord, I thank You that the angel of the Lord is encamping around me and my family and that they deliver us from all our adversaries.

For He shall give His angels charge over you, to keep you in all your ways. In their hands they shall bear you up, lest you dash your foot against a stone.

—Psalm 91:11-12

This scripture has three points of angelic help attached to it.

1. *Angels taking charge over you*—this means they have permission and the responsibility to intervene in circumstances much like a person would reach over and grab a steering wheel to correct a car.

2. *Keep you*—this means they are present at all times and continue watching over you to make sure nothing goes wrong with you.

3. They have permission to *reach out with their hands*—a reference to physically altering a circumstance to rescue or alter something for your benefit. Similar to the time Peter had shackles removed from his hands and feet, or the gates to the prison opened by themselves and Peter walked out. This was the doing of angelic hands.

Thank You, Lord, for charging Your angels over me and my family and that they keep us in all our ways, that Your angels will bear us up, and thank You that we won't get hurt in the process.

*Nebuchadnezzar spoke, saying, "Blessed be the God of Shadrach, Meshach, and Abed-Nego, who sent **His Angel and delivered His servants** who trusted in Him, and **they have frustrated the king's word**, and yielded their bodies, that they should not serve nor worship any god except their own God!"*

—Daniel 3:28

A promise is found here to foil the plans of bad leadership or institutions that set out to do you harm. Angels can frustrate the wrong laws or evil commands for your protection.

> Lord, I call forth Your angels to come and deliver me from every evil situation. I pray that they would frustrate the words of the enemy that are against me.

*And He was there in the wilderness forty days, tempted by Satan, and was with the wild beasts; and **the angels ministered to Him**.*

—Mark 1:13

This Scripture carries the idea that angels can refresh you.

> Lord, I call forth Your ministering angels to come and minister to me, my family, and my loved ones.

273

Or do you think that I cannot now pray to My Father, and **He will provide Me with more than twelve legions of angels?**

—Matthew 26:53

This powerful Scripture holds an understanding of a high-level intervention. You can pray for high-level angelic assistance! As He is, so are we in this world. If Jesus could pray it, so can we.

Thank You, Lord, that just like Jesus knew He could simply pray and ask You to provide Him with many angels, we have that same ability, through Jesus and Your Word, to call forth the assistance of Your angels. In Jesus' name, I call forth Your heavenly legions to assist me in every circumstance!

But at night **an angel of the Lord opened the prison doors** and **brought them out,** *and said, "Go, stand in the temple and speak to the people all the words of this life."*

—Acts 5:19-20

Now behold, an **angel of the Lord stood by him, and a light shone in the prison; and he struck Peter on the side and raised him up,** *saying, "Arise quickly!" And* **his chains fell off his hands.**

—Acts 12:7

Suddenly there was a great earthquake, so that the foundations of the prison were shaken; and immediately all the doors were opened and everyone's chains were loosed.

—**Acts 16:26**

Thank You, Lord, that in moments of desperation, trials, and hardships, You send Your angels to help me in many ways to get out of every situation that is not of You.

I call forth Your angels to go to the aid of (person's name) and help them in whatever way the angels can, so that (name) can get freedom from the situation they are in.

For there stood by me this night an angel of the God to whom I belong and whom I serve.

—**Acts 27:23**

Thank You, Lord, that You have sent Your angel to stand by my side through every difficulty.

Dear reader,

I want you to know that on a bad day you are called to be the best there is. Jesus wants you to win even more than you do, and the above scriptural examples are to help you get started in your prayer journey. Angels will step into action as you rise in praying the promises from the Word of God. I bless you and believe with you, right now, for a complete and total release of everything God has for you. Remember to keep standing in this dark world with the light of God. Speak out the Scriptures in faith, pray in the spirit, and watch angelic assistance work on your behalf! Thank you for taking this journey with me.

For Jesus,
Joseph Z

NOTES

1. Rick Renner, *Dressed to Kill* (Tulsa, OK: Teach All Nations, 2007), Kindle Loc. 2356.

2. F.L. Cross and E.A. Livingstone, eds., *The Oxford Dictionary of the Christian Church* Oxford University Press, s.v. "mysticism, mystical theology," https://www.oxfordreference.com/display/10.1093/acref/9780192802903.001.0001/acref-9780192802903-e-4716?rskey=gGg4lx&result=4712.

3. Cross and Livingstone, *The Oxford Dictionary of the Christian Church*, s.v. "angel," https://www.oxfordreference.com/display/10.1093/acref/9780192802903.001.0001/acref-9780192802903-e-295?rskey=2IRCHC&result=295.

4. Chuck Missler, *Learn the Bible in 24 Hours* (Nashville, TN: Thomas Nelson, 2011), 17-18.

5. Robert Bagley III, *The Book of Enoch* (CreateSpace Independent Publishing Platform, 2016), 3-6.

6. Cross and Livingstone, *The Oxford Dictionary of the Christian Church* s.v. "Books of Enoch," https://www.oxfordreference.com/display/10.1093/acref/9780192802903.001.0001/acref-9780192802903-e-2334?rskey=eSLUmQ&result=2331.

7. This list taken from "Introduction," *The Book of Enoch* by Robert Bagley III.

8. R.H. Charles, trans., *The Book of Enoch* (1917 edition), https://www.sacred-texts.com/bib/boe/index.htm.

9. John Gill, *Gill's Exposition of the Whole Bible*, StudyLight.org, 1 Peter 1:12, https://www.studylight.org/commentaries/eng/geb/1-peter-1.html.

ABOUT JOSEPH Z

J oseph Z is a Bible teacher, author, broadcaster, and international prophetic voice. Before the age of nine, he began encountering the voice of God through dreams and visions. This resulted in a journey that has led him to dedicate his life to the preaching of the gospel and the teaching of the Bible, often followed by prophetic ministry.

For nearly three decades, Joseph planted churches, founded Bible schools, preached stadium events, and held schools of the prophets around the world. Joseph and his wife Heather ministered together for 15 years and made the decision in 2012 to start Z Ministries, a media and conference-based ministry. During this time, they traveled the United States, taking along with them a traveling studio team live broadcasting from a new location several times a week. A season came when Heather became very ill due to hereditary kidney failure. After three years of dialysis and several miracles, she received a miracle kidney transplant. Joseph and Heather decided to stop everything, they laid everything down and ministered to their family for nearly three years.

In 2017 Joseph had an encounter with the Lord and received the word to "go live every weekday morning"—Monday through Friday.

What started with him, Heather, and a small group of viewers, has turned into a large and faithful online broadcast family. Today, his live broadcasts are reaching millions every month with the gospel and current events—which he has labeled "prophetic journalism." He additionally interviews some of the leading voices in the church, government, and the culture.

He and his wife, Heather have two adult children that faithfully work alongside them. Joseph's favorite saying when ending letters, books, or written articles is, "for Jesus." As, "for the testimony of Jesus is the spirit of prophecy." —Revelation 19:10

Joseph spends his time with his family, writing books, broadcasting, and training others in the Word of God.

From

JOSEPH Z

Thriving in God's Supernatural Economy

There's a war being fought over you! The Kingdom of God offers you divine provision while the Kingdom of Hell fights for territory in your life as a crisis looms on the world's horizon.

Will you break free of Hell's economy? International prophet and Bible teacher Joseph Z say it's urgent to break free now as we rapidly plunge into global difficulties involving worldwide market collapse, bank closures, a digital one-world currency, power grids failing, cyber war, medical deception, natural catastrophes, and unprecedented international conflict.

In *Breaking Hell's Economy*, Joseph makes it clear that we're at a destination in history that requires a revelation of God's supernatural economy—your ultimate defense against rising darkness.

Lay hold of this revelation, defy Hell, and live your life knowing you are destined to thrive in the last days!

Purchase your copy wherever books are sold

MINISTRIES
BUILDING LIVES BY THE VOICE OF GOD

Joseph and Heather have ministered together for over 20 years; with a passion to see others be all they are called to be. For many years, Joseph & Heather have had the heart to offer life-changing materials and teaching at no cost to the body of Christ. Today, they have made that a reality by offering various media resources and biblical training free of charge. Joseph and Heather currently reside in Colorado Springs, CO with their two children, Alison and Daniel.

Learn more at
www.josephz.com

For Further Information

If you would like prayer or for further information about Joseph Z Ministries, please call our offices at

(719) 257-8050
or visit **josephz.com/contact**

Visit JosephZ.Com for additional materials

School of the Prophets

School of the prophets is volume 1 of a growing prophetic master course. It includes 39 video sessions with a corresponding manual and audio files. The material inside was developed by Joseph Z from nearly three decades of training believers around the world at conferences and events. This course thoroughly covers the office of the prophet, how you are called to prophesy, dreams, visions, visitations, strange encounters, word of knowledge, predicting the future, deja vu, trances, what society calls empaths, and so much more! You will discover that the Word of God is the final authority on growing your gift of prophecy. This course is not just for prophets but is designed specifically for everyone in the Body of Christ!

Demystifying the Prophetic

Throughout this powerful teaching Joseph Z brings clarity and understanding to things such as déjà vu, multidimensionalism, strange happenings and a variety of common prophetic encounters. Taking a realistic approach in explaining these unique experiences and breaking them down supernaturally as well as scientifically. In part two of this series Joseph Z talks about capacity, leadership, and how not to institutionalize a revelation. You will learn the difference between mature and immature believers function in the voice of God with this BIBLE LOADED teaching!

Archangels - Servants of Fire

Angels have a duty to minister to believers in Jesus, because God has given them charge over us. Your relationship with Angels is highly important as you relate to them through the activated Word of God. They witnessed the fall of Lucifer and know what is in store for mankind. According to the apostle Paul, believers will judge fallen angels. There are many powerful advantages to knowing more about angels. As you listen to this message, prepare to gain biblical knowledge about angels, and to unlock their full potential, for YOUR benefit today!

Surviving a Jacked-Up World

In this series Joseph Z teaches on how to survive and thrive in a world of darkness. He elaborates on how the systems and nations of the world continue to silence and put more demands on the body of Christ. Joseph also highlights historic events that took place when it came to standing for the truth no matter the cost. Explaining how the governing authorities have been sabotaged to fit into the demonic system to usher in the spirit of Antichrist. He expounds on how the Body of Christ has the power to thrive and survive by having Jesus as their Lord which gives them peace, authority, and power to overcome. At the end of this series you will realize that we are called to arise in the boldness and strength of Jesus within us. You will also discover the balance between doing what God wants us to do and obeying the governing authorities.

Anger of Satan

You are the reason Satan transitioned from being Lucifer (an Archangel of glory) into the Devil, History's most vile celestial villain. His hatred for mankind has led him on a strategic rage filled agenda to destroy mankind as the ultimate vengeance toward God for creating mankind. This Series will give you a great understanding of how valuable you are and also the strategy of the Devil to remove from us the understanding of the "COMPLETE GOSPEL". You will learn that the Gospel we have all heard preached is correct but it is not complete until it is working through you. In this series, you will not only learn about Satan and  his origin. You'll uncover the answers to some of the questions you've always had but never asked, and begin a journey of victory, Sonship, and taking your dominion as a free moral agent over the powers of darkness.

Secret To the Life of John

Secret to the Life of John, is a teaching series that will blow the lid off popular fatalist point of views regarding destiny and YOUR quality of life. There was a massive difference between John and all his peers. This difference made a life altering impact on his destiny. His SECRET is so powerful it is a MUST HAVE REVELATION for every believer. YOUR LIFE will be magnificently impacted by the truth found in this series. Get ready to have a paradigm shift in your faith!

Apologetics - Defending the Faith

In a world of uncertainty and many who base their reality on emotion, this series will offer you tools to stand up for what you believe. Apologetics is often misinterpreted to mean an apology. When in fact, the proper definition of apologetics means to have an answer for your faith. It is important to understand that we as believers in the Word of God can be empowered to give confident and reasonable answers to Biblical topics in Love. You will learn some basic thoughts and ideas that will strengthen your confidence in what you believe as well as influence the world around you with truth and power based on the world view of a thinking believer.

Spiritual Warfare

Since the fall of Adam, there has been an ongoing war between the forces of good and evil. Oftentimes, we see free moral agents (humans) being entangled with the agents of darkness and used for nefarious activities. When we hear the phrase 'spiritual warfare', a lot of us have misconceptions about it, fueled by our cultures and age old superstitions. We are all warriors in a war and Christ came to offer us redemption from Satan's captivity. He came to destroy the works of the devil and bring him to nothing. The devil has no power over you and he knows this. Prepare to be enlightened on the dynamics of

spiritual warfare, to enable you to unlock some raw spiritual horsepower that is guaranteed to send Satan and his cronies running.

Wealth of Jesus

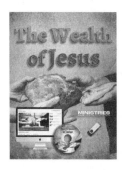

The world wants us to believe that Jesus operated in poverty and lack while on earth. Throughout His days on earth, Jesus was able to meet needs even before they became visible to those around him. All authority has been given to Jesus, both in heaven and on earth. Wealth has never been a concept Jesus operates in because He is above it. Jesus truly mastered wealth and as His representatives, He expects us to do the same. You'll come to learn through this series that Jesus has an endless supply of wealth, but having a knowledge of it is not enough, as God expects us to key into that covenant of wealth!

Stay Connected by Downloading the Joseph Z App

Search "Joseph Z" in your preferred app store.

Uncensored Truth

LIVE Chat

Prophetic Journalism

Real Time Prophetic Ministry

Interviews with Leading Voices

Video Archives

Equipping Believers to Walk in the Abundant Life
John 10:10b

Connect with us for fresh content and news about forthcoming books from your favorite authors...

 Facebook @ HarrisonHousePublishers

Instagram @ HarrisonHousePublishing

www.harrisonhouse.com